SECONDHAND AND VINTAGE

NEW YORK

Debra Johnston Cobb

Vivays Publishing

Published by Vivays Publishing Ltd

www.vivays-publishing.com

A catalogue record for this book is
available from the British Library.

ISBN 978-1-908126-34-4

Publishing Director: Lee Ripley
Editor: Andrew Whittaker
Design: Draught Associates
Cover image: © Sigurd66/Getty Images
Map data: © OpenStreetMap (and) contributors, CC-BY-SA

Printed in China

NEW YORK
CONTENTS

NEW YORK
HOW TO USE THIS BOOK

Secondhand and Vintage New York is organized in four chapters. The first encompasses clothing, jewelry and accessories; the second covers culture, collectibles, memorabilia and mash-ups (stores with a bit of everything); and the third chapter includes home furnishings, lighting and décor. The last chapter, Only in New York, focuses on the city's thrift shops (as New Yorkers call their charity shops), its burgeoning flea market culture, and some of the unique traders associated with the city's manufacturing history.

Within each chapter, the shops and markets are organized by neighborhood, and detailed with contact information, hours of operation, and the nearest subway stop. Small traders can be very independent, and it's never a bad idea to call first and confirm opening hours if you are particularly interested. Each shop is given an indication of pricing from $ to $$$$$; although many shops will have inexpensive items as well as investment pieces. Prices are sometimes negotiable, especially if you are at the flea market or buying multiple or very expensive items; but be respectful and remember you are in New York, not in a bazaar.

The maps in the back of the book are designed to help you shop by neighborhood, with each trader or market noted and color-coded by category/chapter. We've also included some of our favorite local cafés, should you need to rest and refuel. Each map features a QR code link that can be accessed through your smartphone.

Finally, it's worth noting that in the vintage and secondhand business, shops come and go and change location. In addition, the New York subway system is updated every few months, so do check up-to-date subway maps. Every effort was made to confirm the accuracy of these listings at the time the book was written.

INTRODUCTION

When one thinks of New York City, one thinks of a modern metropolis dedicated to progress and all things new. So it comes as a bit of a surprise that New York is in the midst of a love affair with vintage and secondhand shopping and collecting. While the city has always had its share of cheap thrift stores, junky flea markets and dusty antiques shops, since the turn of the millennium the secondhand business has moved into the mainstream, gaining respectability and a host of new fans.

To be truthful, the culture of thriftiness runs deep in New Yorkers. The immigrants of the Lower East Side knew about hand-me-downs, mending and making-do, pushcarts and the rag-and-bone pickers; in 1921 the actress Fanny Brice sang about *Second Hand Rose* in the Ziegfeld Follies. But while the current popularity of secondhand and vintage shopping may be in part attributed to the recession, it seems that New Yorkers are taking more interest in finding well-made, unique clothing and collectibles with personal value; and are seeking to renew and reuse items of good quality, rather than adding to the city's ever-growing refuse pile.

Although secondhand tends to imply 'cheap,' this is not always the case. While there are plenty of inexpensive 'thrift' shops featuring collections of unwanted or donated merchandise, New York also sports a large number of 'consignment' shops selling top-drawer, gently-worn designer clothes. While the prices are less than for new merchandise, secondhand designer goods can still carry a hefty price tag.

Vintage, on the other hand, is not cheap; the value is in the eyes of the beholder. Another word for vintage is 'venerable'; it has an excellence that has survived the passing of time. Vintage shops, with their well-curated collections and knowledgeable keepers, stand apart from the plethora of secondhand sellers.

Thriftiness aside, there's the fun factor involved in browsing through quirky shops or market stalls, delving into dusty bins, or drooling over designer duds.

While many secondhand enclaves and flea markets are found in New York's less familiar neighborhoods, go ahead and explore them. It's the thrill of the hunt, the connection with the past, the sharing with enthusiastic shop owners that makes secondhand and vintage shopping special.

THE NEIGHBORHOODS

Uptown Manhattan
This primarily residential area is home to New York's museums and cultural institutions such as Lincoln Center, with East and West sides separated by lovely Central Park.

Midtown West/Chelsea
While Chelsea has long been established as an artsy enclave, the recent renovation of the New York Central Railroad's High Line as a pedestrian park has spurred gentrification along Manhattan's more industrial West Side, home to the city's renowned garment center.

Gramercy Park/Thrift Row
The privately-owned Gramercy Park on East 20th Street is surrounded by Victorian townhouses, and is one of the prettiest squares in the city. A few blocks north, several of the city's best thrift shops are clustered along East 23rd Street.

East Village/NoHo/Greenwich Village
Historic Greenwich Village in the west gives way at Broadway to the more bohemian East Village and Alphabet City, where prices are more appropriate to its student and artist population.

SoHo/Nolita/Tribeca
The neighborhood's old cast-iron factories and warehouses became home to artists' lofts and galleries, and the area is now a center for international high-end retail therapy.

Lower East Side
The tenements of the Lower East Side housed waves of immigrants and the neighborhood is the historic center of American Jewish culture; while trendy boutiques and restaurants have moved in, the area is now preserved by the National Trust for Historic Preservation.

Downtown Brooklyn
Brooklyn's downtown neighborhoods range from the industrial Gowanus to the beautifully preserved Clinton Hill, along with family neighborhoods such as Boerum Hill, Park Slope, Cobble Hill and Carroll Gardens; these are easily accessible via the transportation hub that is the Atlantic Avenue station.

Williamsburg, Brooklyn
In the 1970s creative types from lower Manhattan began moving to old industrial Williamsburg in search of lower rents. Since then the neighborhood has become the home of the hip, with vintage and independent boutiques, bars and restaurants that are no longer cheap. Take the East River Ferry (www.nywaterway.com/ERF) from Manhattan to the Williamsburg waterfront for great views.

CLOTHES & ACCESSORIES

Men's, Women's, and Children's Garments / Hats / Bags and Belts / Shoes / Jewelry / Watches / Eyeglasses

FROM THE HAND-ME-DOWNS OF THE LOWER EAST SIDE TO THE CHARITABLE CASTOFFS OF UPTOWN SOCIETY, NEW YORKERS HAVE LONG BEEN FAMILIAR WITH SECONDHAND CLOTHING. BUT IT WASN'T UNTIL THE BOHEMIAN ARTISTS AND STUDENTS OF THE 1950S AND 60S TOOK TO DRESSING IN WORKMAN'S BLUE JEANS, BOYFRIEND SWEATERS AND RECYCLED MILITARY PARAPHERNALIA THAT SECONDHAND CLOTHING WAS CONSIDERED COOL BY THE INTELLECTUAL FRINGE. DURING THE LATE 60S AND EARLY 70S THE 'REVOLUTIONARIES' OF THE COUNTER-CULTURE MIXED ETHNIC AND INDIGENOUS DESIGNS WITH BITS FROM THEIR GRANDPARENTS' CLOSETS; AND THE MOVIE *ANNIE HALL* SHOWED US HOW TO PUT IT ALL TOGETHER.

By the time I moved to New York in the mid-70s, vintage shops such as Reminiscence and Screaming Mimi's were featured in the fashion magazines; those of us on a budget discovered the joys of thrift shops such as the Salvation Army. New York vintage style truly came into its own in the new millennium, via Patricia Field's mix of old and new for the television show *Sex and the City*; while celebrities began to search out vintage designer looks for their red carpet appearances.

New York now offers vintage and secondhand fashion from all eras, at all price points, from the posh consignment shops of the Upper East Side, to the rummage-sale atmosphere of the downtown thrifts. Swap shops are a recent development; bring in your currently fashionable but unwanted treasures for the store to sell, and if they are accepted you receive cash or store credit and can immediately choose something from the racks to take home. Creating new from old or 'upcycling' is another growing trend, as independent designers rework, recycle, or repurpose vintage pieces and dead stock.

In between you'll find shops where true vintage enthusiasts collect, curate, and share their passion with their customers. You never know where you are going to find the special garment, handbag, shoes, or jewelry that brings the past alive for you.

$ $ $ $

A SECOND CHANCE

1109 Lexington Avenue, 2nd floor,
Upper East Side 10075
212-744-6041
www.asecondchanceresale.com
Mon-Fri 11:00-19:00; Sat 11:00-18:00
Subway 4, 5, 6 to 86th Street,
or 6 to 77th Street

Owned and run by a mother-daughter
team who carefully hand select the
pre-loved, consignment designer wear
on sale, this spacious two-room boutique
is known for its amazing array of status
bags, shoes and baubles. Think Vuitton
luggage, a Gucci ostrich bag, a collection
of Hermès' Kellys and Birkins, classic
quilted Chanels, and recent must-have
bags from YSL and Prada. Upper East Side
ladies love their Chanel, and the collection
of suits and jewelry here won't disappoint.
With a second boutique down in SoHo,
this is secondhand shopping at a
rarified level.

Other location:
155 Prince Street, 10012 (212-673-6155)

$⑤⑤⑤
BIS DESIGNER RESALE

1134 Madison Avenue, 2nd floor,
Upper East Side 10028
212-396-2760
www.bisbiz.com
Mon-Sat 10:00-18:00 (Thu to 19:00);
Sun 12:00-17:00
Subway 4, 5, 6 to 86th Street

Bis is one flight up from the street
level, where Henri Dauman and his
knowledgeable staff will make you feel
welcome in their world of women's
consignment designer fashions. The
carefully selected, high-end merchandise
includes 'pre-loved' pieces from the likes
of Leger, de la Renta, Armand Basi, Marni
and Thakoon; perfect for special occasion
dressing. There's also a nice collection
of jewelry, Judith Leiber bags and
oversized designer sunglasses from
Gucci, Chanel, etc.

$⑤⑤⑤⑤
ENCORE

1132 Madison Avenue, 2nd floor,
Upper East Side 10028
212-879-2850
www.encoreresale.com
Mon-Sat 10:30-18:30 (Thu to 19:30);
Sun 12:00-18:00
Subway 4, 5, 6 to 86th Street

This well-established consignment shop
(since 1954) for women's fashion may not
be cheap, but the up-to-date, designer-
name merchandise is pristine. Racks of
day dresses from Miu Miu, Pucci, Herrera,
Oscar de la Renta and Vera Wang are
organized by size, along with a rack of
smart little black cocktail dresses. There's
also a great selection of Chanel jackets, an
Upper East Side staple. You can top your
purchase off with a designer fur or coat
by the likes of Prada and Montcler.
Smart, well-heeled ladies shop here.

$ $ $ $

LA BOUTIQUE RESALE

1045 Madison Avenue, 2nd floor,
Upper East Side 10075
212-517-8099
jon@laboutiqueresale.com
www.laboutiqueresale.com
Mon-Sat 10:30-19:00; Sun 11:00-18:30
Subway 4, 5, 6 to 86th Street,
or 6 to 77th Street

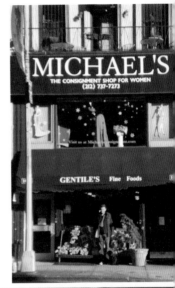

With a younger point-of-view and more
true vintage merchandise than other
consignment shops, 15-year-old La
Boutique actually has three locations in
the tony Upper East Side. There's a fine
selection of gently-worn, current high-
end fashion from the likes of Prada, Marc
Jacobs, Burberry, Stella McCartney, Max
Mara, Diane Von Furstenberg, Tory Burch,
Paul & Joe, etc., along with Manolos,
Louboutins and Jimmy Choos, and
precious Vuitton and Hermès bags. The
Chanel rack will take your breath away,
and a well-priced rack of candy-colored
cashmere sweaters is a sweet treat.
Vintage selections include Pucci jerseys,
Mad Men cocktail dresses, fur-collared
brocade dinner suits and swishy opera
capes. The shop is a fave among the red
carpet crowd, who "cleaned out the place"
for the Obama inauguration a few years
back, according to owner Jonathan.

Other locations:
141 East 62nd Street, 2nd floor, 10065
(212-517-8099)

227 East 81st Street, 10028 (212-988-8188)

Ⓢ Ⓢ Ⓢ Ⓢ

MICHAEL'S

1041 Madison Avenue, 2nd floor,
Upper East Side 10075
212-737-7273
www.michaelsconsignment.com
Mon-Sat 09:30-18:00 (Thu to 20:00)
(Sun closed; Sat/Sun in July/Aug closed)
Subway 4, 5, 6 to 86th Street,
or 6 to 77th Street

Michael's is a New York institution with
its roots in the Lower East Side, where
Simon Kosofsky had a secondhand shop
in the late 19th century. His son, Aaron,
founded the legendary Ritz Furs shop
(see p18) in the 1940s, and grandson
Michael opened the Madison Avenue
consignment shop for high fashion in
1954. The merchandise is organized by
brand and features the crème de la crème
of gently-used (and sometimes never
worn) designer merchandise, including
enough Chanel suits, dresses and coats
and Manolo Blahnik shoes to make a girl
weep. Michael's is still managed by family,
who ensure every designer treasure is
authentic and in pristine condition.

Ⓢ Ⓢ

BUFFALO EXCHANGE

114 West 26th Street, Chelsea 10001
212-675-3535
contact@bufex.com
www.buffaloexchange.com
Mon-Sat 11:00-20:00; Sun 12:00-19:00
Subway 1, F, M, N, R to 23rd Street,
or 1, N, R to 28th Street

A consignment shop with a conscience,
the Buffalo Exchange philosophy
encompasses buying, selling and trading
unworn and gently-used, contemporary
clothing – recycling on a local basis to
keep fast fashion out of the landfill. The
Chelsea store, one of three NYC locations,
is clean, tidy and well merchandised;
clothing styles are primarily for the young
and hip, who bring in their castoffs in
exchange for cash or store credit. H&M,
French Connection, Club Monaco, Banana
Republic, Tommy Hilfiger, Vineyard
Vines and Burberry are regularly found
on the racks. Shoes are a strong point; we
snapped up a pair of gold Lanvin sandals
for a song, and spotted a pair of Calvin
Klein men's oxfords at a great price. There
are also top-brand men's kicks (trainers)
such as Nike and Vans; along with cheap
sunglasses and costume bangles to
accessorize any look.

Other locations:
332 East 11th Street, 10003 (212-260-9340)

504 Driggs Avenue, Williamsburg,
Brooklyn 11211 (718-384-6901)

THE FAMILY JEWELS

130 West 23rd Street, Chelsea 10011
212-633-6020
chelseagirl@familyjewelsnyc.com
www.familyjewelsnyc.com
Mon-Sun 11:00-19:00
Subway 1, F, M to 23rd Street

A favorite of designers, stylists and celebrities for its collection of American vintage, this 2000 square-foot store was established in 1980 and features a well-curated selection of clothing for men and women, from late Victoriana to 80s synthetics. There are wedding gowns, beaded flapper dresses, and 1950s cocktail dresses; pretty printed cotton day dresses; and smart silk sheaths from the 60s. The smart-dressed man can choose from vintage tuxedos, smoking jackets, double-breasted suits and pleated trousers in fabric favorites such as silk, sharkskin, gabardine or seersucker. Bowling shirts from the 50s, polyester fashion from the 70s, vintage leather jackets and accessories ranging from shoes to bow ties complete his ensemble. Clothing is tagged by era and waist size for convenience. In addition, the store carries hats, bags, gloves, and jewelry; along with retro lingerie, kitchen kitsch, doilies and embroidered dresser scarves, and some charming children's clothing.

FISCH FOR THE HIP

153 West 18th Street, Chelsea 10011
212-633-9053
www.fischforthehip.com
Mon-Sat 12:00-19:00; Sun 12:00-18:00
Subway 1 to 18th Street,
or F, M to 14th Street or 23rd Street

This high-end consignment shop stocks only the best in recent and barely-worn designer garb for men and women, along with shoes and bags to die for. Where else can you find an entire wall of Hermès' Kelly and Birkin bags, Prada and Chanel bags, Manolos and Jimmy Choos? While there's a bit of attitude in the air, owner Terin Tischer's impeccable eye is the reason the shop's been in existence for over 20 years.

PIPPIN VINTAGE JEWELRY

💲💲💲

112 West 17th Street, Chelsea 10011
212-505-5159
info@pippinvintage.com
www.pippinvintage.com
Mon-Sat 11:00-19:00; Sun 12:00-18:00
Subway F, M to 14th Street,
or L to Sixth Avenue, or 1 to 18th Street

This gem of a store is named for owners Rachel and Steve Cooper's dog and was established in 2005 on Manhattan's Lower East Side before moving to its present location. There's a wide selection of costume jewelry from the mid 19th century to the 1970s, artfully displayed in antique cases or across pretty tables, bureaus and dresser scarves. Most pieces are reasonably priced, from cufflinks and tie clips to Victorian hair brooches and Bakelite jewelry; although the Art Deco platinum watches are a bit more precious. Clip earrings and strands of beads will remind you of playing with your mom's jewelry box, and there are hats, bags and hankies for ladylike accessorizing. Next door find Pippin Vintage Home (see p87), with furniture and home goods, as well as some more modern jewelry.

REMINISCENCE

💲💲

50 West 23rd Street, Chelsea 10010
212-243-2292
contactus@reminiscence.com
www.reminiscence.com
Mon-Sat 11:00-19:30; Sun 12:00-19:00
Subway F, M, N, R to 23rd Street

Founded in 1975, Reminiscence was one of New York's early vintage outposts, with racks of secondhand jeans, military dead stock, and early psychedelia. While you'll still find leather, lace, and some Hawaiian shirts from the 50s through the 80s, much of the merchandise includes 'retro-inspired' gift items; but it's lots of fun.

RITZ FURS

$$$$

345 Seventh Avenue, 9th Floor,
Midtown West 10001
212-265-4559
ritzfurs@ritzfurs.com
www.ritzfurs.com
Mon-Sat 10:00-17:30
(Sat in July closed; Aug closed)
Subway 1, 2, 3 to 34th Street,
or 1 to 28th Street

As an underpaid young fashion editor in
1970s New York, I coveted the fur coats
worn by the city's chic women. Then I
discovered the Ritz Thrift Shop, where
"you don't have to spend a million to look
like a million!" Established in 1934, the
Ritz Thrift Shop spent over 60 years on
57th Street selling the 'gently-worn' furs
of the city's elite on consignment. In 2005,
it became Ritz Furs, moving to Seventh
Avenue in the midst of the city's former
fur district, where pelts and fur garments
used to be wholesaled. While the company
now offers new furs as well, it's the pre-
loved pieces that make Ritz Furs unique.
There are vintage stoles, wraps and hats
from the 1950s and 60s, colorful fun-fur
chubbies from the 70s, and glamorous full-
length minks. The secondhand inventory
also includes sable, beaver and fox, all at
prices well below what you'd pay for a new
fur. If you are visiting in the summer, call
ahead to confirm hours.

SHAREEN VINTAGE

$$$

13 West 17th Street, 2nd floor, Chelsea 1001
212-206-1644
shareen@Shareenvintage.com
www.shareenvintage.com
Wed-Fri 13:00-21:00; Sat 14:00-18:00;
or by appointment
Subway 4, 5, 6, N, R, Q, L to Union Square,
or F, M to 14th Street or 23rd Street

On a side street in Chelsea a red gown
hangs on the fire escape of an old
apartment building, your only indication
of the second-floor walkup that is Shareen
Vintage's New York store. Girls just
wanna have fun – and no boys allowed
– at this outpost of LA-based vintage
stylist, designer and TV presenter
Shareen Mitchell, where you can play
dress-up with modern vintage that is
"not preserved but meant to be worn and
styled." With a warehouse in Los Angeles
the merchandise is slanted towards LA
funky from the 1950s forward, including
reasonably priced day dresses. Shareen
also designs a line of 'upcycled' garments
starting with dresses from the iconic 1970
Gunne Sax line by Jessica McClintock.
The shop specializes in occasion dressing
with vintage bridal gowns and beaded
cocktail and evening wear; and customer
are invited to reserve the premises for
celebratory shopping parties. The staff
doesn't just sell, but helps style your look

⑤⑤

ANGELA'S VINTAGE BOUTIQUE

330 East 11th Street, East Village 10003
212-475-1571
Mon-Sun 12:00-20:00
Subway L to First Avenue, or 6 to Astor Place

Specializing in after-five looks from the
1920s through the 1980s, Angela's has
plenty of tulle and sequins, as well as
1950s sundresses and lacy shifts from
the 60s. A smart collection of felt cloches
from the 20s, period bags, shoes and
accessories, and select fur pieces create
a real retro feel.

⑤⑤

AUH₂O THRIFTIQUE

84 East Seventh Street, East Village 10003
212-466-0844
auh2oshop@gmail.com
www.auh2oshop.com
Mon-Sun 12:00-20:00
Subway L to First Avenue, or 6 to Astor Place

Just in case you skipped chemistry class,
AuH_2O is the symbol for goldwater;
founders Kate Goldwater and Alexandra
Sinderbrand describe themselves as
"addicted to the thrill of the hunt" and
"dirt cheap." The friends cull estate sales
and warehouses for women's apparel,
shoes and accessories; a great selection of
vintage jewelry is sourced from a supplier
or reworked by eco-conscious Kate.
While the shop is small and the selection
fueled by pretty dresses and funky prints,
the bottom line is cute clothes in great
condition at reasonable prices.

§§
BEST OF RYLEY INC

345 Lafayette, NoHo 10012
610-724-7983
www.brownyintl.com
Mon-Fri 10:00-20:00; Sat/Sun 11:00-20:00
Subway B, D, F, M to Broadway-Lafayette,
or 6 to Bleecker Street

A charming jumble of quirky bric-a-brac,
exotic and girly jewelry, and globally-
sourced vintage clothing at realistic
prices; this relatively new shop is a great
find. Designer and collector Julie Erinc
reworks and hand-dyes secondhand
wedding and prom gowns to create
the kind of looks coveted by indie rock
musicians (think Florence Welch). Wear
them with the shop's pretty bits of vintage
lingerie and layers of pendants and
bracelets from previous decades. There
are tables strewn with perfume bottles, tea
sets, shot glasses, cufflinks, stylish hats,
and old dressmaking patterns; as well
as tableware and textiles imported from
Turkey and Afghanistan.

§§§
CADILLAC'S CASTLE

333 East Ninth Street, East Village 10003
212-475-0406
cadillacscastle@verizon.net
Mon-Sun 12:00-20:00
Subway L to First Avenue, or 6 to Astor Place

Selling gently-worn, uptown fashion on
consignment, but without the uptown
attitude, Cadillac's Castle is a bright and
pretty little store with whitewashed brick
walls and pebble floors. Flirty dresses,
chic shoes, bags, and accessories from
contemporary designers will satisfy the
fashionista with more dash than cash;
some of the items still sport their
original tags.

Best of Ryley Inc: The Erinc sisters

Sisters Ayshe (right) and Aylin (left) have inherited their mother Julie's sense of style, and their Turkish father's appreciation for travel and the arts and crafts of other cultures. They shop estate sales, flea markets and designer collectives, contributing to Best of Ryley's atmosphere of bohemian chic. They describe their mother as a bit of a hoarder: "She actually has her own warehouse. If you were to see our house – it is so cluttered you can't walk." We say: more, please.

COBBLESTONES

314 East Ninth Street, East Village 10003
212-673-5372
Tues-Sun 13:00-19:00
Subway L to First Avenue, or 6 to Astor Place

East Village native Delanee Koppersmith grew up with a mom who was a collector and "always wanted a store," and brings a real respect for classic vintage to her 30-year-old boutique. Part consignment, part thrift shop, Cobblestones reflects the glamour of the 30s, 40s and 50s; clothing is tagged by era, and big band music plays in the background. "I have the privilege of knowing a lot of senior citizens who like to see their belongings appreciated," says Delanee, "and I love their stories of New York." We loved the mid-century satin bras and a great selection of 60s and 70s clothing in pop-art colors and patterns. Shoes are displayed on a wall grid for easy access; hats are a strongpoint; and there's a lovely assortment of framed needlepoint and beaded handbags.

DUO

337 East Ninth Street, East Village 10003
212-777-7044
duo@duonyc.com
www.duonyc.com
Mon-Sun 12:30-20:30
Subway L to First Avenue, or 6 to Astor Place

This lovely shop with its creaky wooden flooring, antique light fixtures and brick fireplace features the best of vintage and modern clothing and accessories for women by emerging local designers, edited by sisters Wendy and LaRae Kangas. Vintage clothing harks from the 1890s to the 1980s, and the selection is updated weekly; the shoes here get especially high marks.

§§

DUSTY BUTTONS

441 East Ninth Street, East Village 10009
212-673-4039
dusty@dustybuttons.com
www.dustybuttons.com
Tues-Fri 12:00-20:00; Sat 12:00-19:00;
Sun 12:00-18-00
Subway L to First Avenue, or 6 to Astor Place

Yes, there is a real Dusty Buttons, and her
enthusiasm for pretty vintage dressing
is infectious, as is her love for the East
Village vibe. Like many shops in the
neighborhood, Dusty mixes vintage and
new clothing, shoes, housewares, and odds
and ends; and does her own research and
buying. While she particularly admires
the aesthetics of authentic 1930s to 80s
vintage, what's most important is that
her girls have fun.

§§

ELEVEN CONSIGNMENT BOUTIQUE

180 First Avenue, East Village 10009
212-260-2742
Mon-Wed 10:00-22:00; Thu-Sat 10:00-
23:00; Sun 11:00-20:00
Subway L to First Avenue, or 6 to Astor Place

This compact and well-organized shop
stands out for its high quality stock at
excellent prices, and the owners are
clearly choosy about the merchandise
they buy, sell, trade and rent. We found
a ladies' Marni top and a Shanghai Tang
velvet vest; with lots more current and
vintage designer names ranging from
Cynthia Steffe to John Weitz. For guys,
there are suits and sports clothes by the
likes of Paul Smith, Barneys New York
and Rag & Bone. A well-edited selection of
designer denims, plus designer shoes and
accessories, makes this East Village gem a
favorite of stylists and editors.

$⑤$$⑤$

LADIES & GENTLEMEN

338 East 11th Street, East Village 10003
hello@ladiesandgentlemennyc.com
www.ladiesandgentlemennyc.com
Mon-Sun 13:00-20:00
Subway L to First Avenue, or 6 to Astor Place

This newcomer to the East Village vintage scene offers a choice assortment of authentic men's workwear and Americana culled from the owners' personal collection. Cases full of vintage watches and class rings, bandanas, belts and suspenders, ties and eyeglass frames are a pleasure to browse, while vintage rock star posters and old American flags line the walls. There's a great selection of well-loved wingtips, deck shoes, workboots, motorcycle boots and Converse Chuck Taylors from the 50s, 60s and 70s, along with heritage Hudson Bay and Pendleton blankets, traditional Pendleton and Woolrich plaid shirts, Native American-inspired vests and jackets, and cozy varsity jackets and sweaters. Secondhand pieces from Belstaff, Barbour, Filson, Coach, Polo Ralph Lauren, Brooks Bros, and some vintage Japanese items add to the utilitarian aura.

$⑤$$⑤$

FABULOUS FANNY'S

335 East Ninth Street, East Village 10003
212-533-0637
fabulousfannys@verizon.net
www.fabulousfannys.com
Mon-Sun 12:00-20:00
Subway L to First Avenue, or 6 to Astor Place

Fanny's specializes in vintage and one-of-a-kind eyewear; their motto is "if you have to wear them, make it fun." You'll find specs from early 19th century wire-rimmed ovals and pince-nez to driving goggles, cat's-eye and butterfly rims, along with designer shades from the 1960s through the 1980s; all displayed on antique dressers and cabinets. Prices are amazingly modest – on par with contemporary designer frames – and you can have your vintage frames customized with rhinestones. Owner Stanton Blackmer started the business in the West 25th Street Flea Market with a box of frames from his mother's New Hampshire store, and claims the oldest eyewear in his collection dates back to the 1700s. The shop features men's and women's clothing and accessories as well, including a smart collection of pillbox hats.

$$$$ LIMITED SUPPLY

273 East Tenth Street, East Village 10009
212-260-3653
Mon-Sun 11:00-20:00
Subway L to First Avenue, or 6 to Astor Place

Opened in 2009, this consignment shop is set apart by the contemporary taste level of its owner, Armani Exchange accessories designer Yevgeniy Tsarkov. Small and bright, with white brick walls and bleached wood floors, the store's stock is primarily modern, designer-level sportswear for both men and women. The men's collection is particularly impressive, including Prada jackets, Paul Smith shirts and Hermès and Brioni ties. There's an assortment of pretty, less-ubiquitous women's handbags, as well as shoes, costume jewelry and other accessories.

ⓈⓈⓈ

MATIELL

350 East Ninth Street, East Village 10003
212-477-1123
matiellconsign350@hotmail.com
Mon-Sun 12:30-20:00
Subway L to First Avenue, or 6 to Astor Place

One of many designer consignment
shops in the East Village, Matiell features
clothing for both men and women. Coats,
suits, dresses and accessories from the
likes of Prada, Von Furstenberg and
Nanette Lepore are moderately priced.

ⓈⓈⓈⓈ

MINA

32A Cooper Square, East Village 10003
212-253-5894
info@minanyc.com
www.minanyc.com
Mon-Sat 11:00-19:00; Sun 12:00-18:00
Subway N, R to Eighth Street,
or 6 to Astor Place

Mina is the resale outlet for the Albright
Fashion Library, a 7000 square-foot loft a
few doors away housing a mind-boggling
array of designer gowns, occasion dresses
and shoes that have been collected and
catalogued by New York stylist Irene
Albright and her daughter Marina. While
the Albright Fashion Library rents its
beautiful fashion pieces to stylists and
the glitterati for fashion shoots, movies
and red carpet events, Mina sells off its
past-prime merchandise to would-be
Cinderellas for a song. The warehouse-like
space is full of recent red carpet looks;
along with a vast selection of nearly-new
shoes worn by runway models in the
seasonal fashion shows.

💲💲

NO RELATION VINTAGE

204 First Avenue, East Village 10009
212-228-5201
www.norelationvintage.com
Mon-Thu 13:00-20:00; Fri 13:00-21:00; Sat
12:00-21:00; Sun 12:00-20:00
Subway L to First Avenue, or 6 to Astor Place

With prices well-suited to the denizens of downtown, No Relation Vintage is a good-and-plenty jumble of casualwear for both men and women. The merch is primarily from the 60s to 80s era, culled from Midwestern warehouses, with just enough out-of-fashion irony to be cool. Men's pea coats starting at $75 are a staple for New York's windy winter streets; and there are leather jackets, army parkas, and fur coats as well. Amidst the flannel shirts, vintage rag jumpers and Fair Isle-patterned sweaters, graphic tees, duck shoes, and Doc Martens, you'll find some pretty dresses, promwear, and plaid sports jackets.

💲💲💲

REASON OUTPOST

436 East Ninth Street, East Village 10009
212-228-7030
info@reasonclothing.com
www.reasonclothing.com
Mon-Sun 12:00-20:00
Subway L to First Avenue, or 6 to Astor Place

Outpost is the flagship of New York menswear line Reason Clothing, established in 2004. The line's T-shirts, knitwear, work jackets and cotton trousers are inspired by – and mixed with – an assortment of real Americana and vintage items from Japan and Europe, housed in a cozy setting reminiscent of an old general store. Old farm implements, hand-painted signs, taxidermy, and antique furnishings complement the store's dark wood fittings. Vintage for sale includes rock tour tees, hunting and military jackets, Carhartt workwear, Pendleton flannel shirts, cameras, bags, wallets and shoes.

Shopping for vintage in NYC

THIS IS HOW TO GET IT

We spotted Soho hairdressers Kathryn Gardner and Christopher Zelasko, who love buying vintage and secondhand, at Village Style. "I've loved it since I was a teenager," she tells us. The two shop mostly in the East Village and Brooklyn, claiming that the prices and selections are better than elsewhere. "It's more fun to find pieces that nobody else will have," says Christopher. "Vintage lasts longer because the fabrics are better," adds Kathryn. The friends clearly know how to assemble an ensemble.

A GENTLEMAN IN NEW YORK

Reg Wang is a sartorially-savvy young man who went to college in the UK midlands, and now attends New York University where he is studying psychology. We found him going through the vintage clothes at Ladies & Gentleman in the East Village. He likes to research and collect good quality clothing that is functional and stands the test of time. "I don't like things that are flash and over with quickly," he says as he shows off the Belstaff jacket he has just purchased. "Here you can buy English stuff cheap."

RUE ST. DENIS

170 Avenue B, East Village 10009
212-260-3388
www.vintagenyc.com
Mon-Fri 12:00-20:00; Sat/Sun 12:00-19:00
Subway L to First Avenue, or 6 to Astor Place

This veteran of the vintage trade moved downtown with the times in 1993 after three years on the Upper West Side, and is known for its large selection of unworn or 'dead stock' designer vintage from the 1940s through the 1980s, often with the original tickets still attached. The European owners – Jean-Paul is French, Ricardo is Italian – have a flair for menswear, and their selection of classic three-piece suits, skinny suits from the 60s, polyester leisure suits and flared trousers from the 70s, and gently patina'd leather motorcycle jackets, is arguably the best in the city. Women's clothing is smart and chic, with a Parisian attitude: silky printed blouses, cocktail and day dresses, Harris tweed and camel hair jackets, and fur-collared coats. Tasteful shoes, boots, and accessories are of good quality – no trainers here, please – and prices are appropriate. A note to the price-conscious: the shop's old stock is occasionally sold off at Brooklyn Flea for around a third of the retail price.

RENA REBORN

117 East Seventh Street, East Village 10009
212-253-2595
info@renareborn.com
www.renareborn.com
Mon-Sat 11:00-20:00; Sun 12:00-18:00
Subway L to First Avenue, or 6 to Astor Place

Rena is the Latin word for reborn, and owner Rachael Rush describes her boutique as "a new way to think of recycled fashion." The shop is a mix of vintage, refashioned and new clothing, and accessories from local designers, all at very good prices. Most of the secondhand stock is from the 1970s and later; the refashioned items have a one-of-a-kind cachet; and the delicate jewelry is particularly good. Racks of marked-down clearance items and student discounts make this a very affordable experience.

SCREAMING MIMI'S

382 Lafayette Street, NoHo 10003
212-677-6464
sales@screamingmimis.com
www.screamingmimis.com
Mon-Sat 12:00-20:00; Sun 13:00-19:00
Subway 6 to Bleecker Street or Astor Place,
or N, R to Eighth Street

An early trendsetter in the New York
vintage scene that emerged in the late
1970s, Screaming Mimi's still echoes
the era's cheerful bohemian vibe with
its period wallpaper and assortment of
mid-to-late-century dress-up. Clothes are
arranged by the decade; there are satin
cone bras from the 1950s, embroidered
shifts from the 1960s, patchworked and
paisley'd long skirts from the 1970s, and
jumpsuits and lame stretch pants from
the 1980s. Men's vintage includes fringed
suede pieces, sheepskin jackets, paisley
shirts, patchworked and beaded vests,
and doubleknit ensembles. Mix in piles of
plastic jewelry, platform shoes, sunglasses,
gloves, goth and punk stuff, the occasional
designer piece, and the prerequisite bell-
bottom denims for a good time. You'll
leave smiling.

STOCK VINTAGE

143 East 13th Street, East Village 10003
212-505-2505
Mon-Fri 12:00-20:00; Sat 12:00-19:00;
Sun 12:00-18:00
Subway 4, 5, 6, N, Q, R, L to 14th Street
Union Square, or L to Third Avenue

Specializing in authentic Americana
and rustic menswear, this shop evokes
an Adirondack camp store with its old
wooden floor and weathered fixtures.
Don't come here looking for trendy;
instead think steel-toed workboots, bibbed
overalls, flannel and denim workshirts,
Quality Mills knitted vests, camp T-shirts,
and a wall of beautifully-tooled belts.
Established in 2006, Stock Vintage
reflects an early 20th century American
aesthetic that contrasts nicely with more
typical vintage collections.

$ $ $

TOKIO7

83 East Seventh Street, East Village 10003
212-353-8443
www.tokio7.net
Mon-Sun 12:00-20:00
Subway L to First Avenue, or 6 to Astor Place

Don't be frightened by the giant robot guarding the door of Tokio7; inside this big and bright consignment shop, established in 1995, is a cutting-edge assortment of designer clothing for men and women. The gently-worn merchandise includes names such as Chanel, Prada, Gucci, Dolce & Gabbana, Marni, See by Chloe, and Japanese brands such as Issey Miyake and Yohji Yamamoto, as well as upscale denims, coats and jackets. The men's selection is especially good here, including Paul Smith, Gucci and Versace dress shirts; we particularly liked a range of waistcoats, as well as some Jeremy Scott for Adidas kicks (trainers). If the prices seem high for the neighborhood, remember that it's designer consignment.

$ $

TOKYO JOE

334 East 11th Street, East Village 10003
212-473-0724
Mon-Sun 12:00-21:00
Subway L to First Avenue, or 6 to Astor Place

Hipper and less expensive than the uptown consignment shops, Tokyo Joe specializes in pretty, girly things such as cute printed skirts and silky or lacy tops by uptown faves including Tory Burch, Carolina Herrera, Cynthia Steffe, Alice + Olivia, and Marc Jacobs. There are lots of totes and handbags, a decent selection of shoes, and men's dress shirts as well.

$

VILLAGE STYLE

111 East Seventh Street, East Village 10009
212-260-6390
www.villagestyleny.com
Mon-Thu 13:00-21:00; Fri/Sat 12:00-22:00;
Sun 12:00-20:00
Subway L to First Avenue, or 6 to Astor Place

There are designer vintage shops, and then there are the places where village hipsters and students go for bargains. Village Style is the latter, offering a large selection of secondhand and consignment basics, bags and footwear for men and women in an unassuming setting. The basics are good and inexpensive: T-shirts and jeans, suede and leather jackets, pea coats, flannel shirts, lumberjack plaids, funky faux furs, and great cowboy and rocker boots. You might even score Prada shoes, a prom dress, or something glittery and fabulous.

$$$

VOZ

618 East Ninth Street, East Village 10009
646-845-9618
info@voznewyork.com
www.voznewyork.com
Mon-Sat 12:00-19:00; Sun 12:00-18:00
Subway L to First Avenue, or 6 to Astor Place

Part vintage collection, part consignment shop, VOZ is more like a gallery of beautifully eclectic women's fashion, curated by owners and former fashion industry designers Naoko Ito and Alex de Laxalt. The two travel the world in search of upscale vintage clothing from Europe, Japan and the US. The merchandise includes real vintage finds such as Victorian lace pieces, beaded gowns from the 1920s and 1930s, eyelet and piqué dresses from the 1950s, crochet and jersey dresses from the 1970s, and sportswear from the 1980s; and while the concrete floor is pasted over with pages from an old Webster's dictionary, there are no cobwebs here – the presentation mixes old with new. Pre-loved shoes, handbags and jewelry are primarily modern-era.

VOZ:
A SENSE
OF
BALANCE

Born in Japan, Naoko Ito came to the US
in 1997, where she worked for New York
design houses Perry Ellis and Generra;
and for Nanette Lepore, where she was the
fabric buyer. It was at Perry Ellis where
she met her business partner, Alex de
Laxalt; and the two opened VOZ in 2009.

The word voz is Spanish for voice, and
VOZ expresses the harmony between
the shop's owners, as well as the balance
found in its combination of vintage and
modern styles.

NAOKO HAS BEEN
COLLECTING
'VINTAGE' SINCE
BEFORE IT BECAME
FASHIONABLE.

Her mother was a designer in Japan, "So
I grew up with good clothes, things that
were not mass produced," she explains.
"I appreciate good quality – there are
some things I would never want to sell."

$ $ $

THE CLOTHING WAREHOUSE

8 Prince Street, Nolita 10012
212-343-1967
www.theclothingwarehouse.com
Mon-Thu 11:30-19:00; Fri/Sat 11:30-20:00;
Sun 12:00-19:00
Subway 6 to Spring Street, J, M, Z to Bowery,
or F, V to Second Avenue

This Atlanta-based chain brings Southern girl casual and vintage Americana to New York, including the best collection of secondhand cowboy boots in the city, along with authentic American denim jeans and jackets, leather jackets and belts, Western shirts, boho skirts and retro tees. Owners Jim Buckley and Erin Faulman have a wholesale and franchise vintage business as well, resulting in a constant flow of great "modern American vintage" merchandise. Prices are reasonable, and bartering is acceptable here.

$ $ $

FREITAG

1 Prince Street, Nolita 10012
212-334-0928
nyc@freitag.ch
www.freitag.ch
Tues-Sun 11:00-19:00 (Thu to 21:00)
Subway 6 to Spring Street, J, M, Z to Bowery,
or F, V to Second Avenue

Made in Zurich, this good-looking line of utilitarian bags may be familiar to Europeans, but the recently opened NYC store suits the city's current passion for recycled and repurposed merchandise. Colorful, water-repellent Freitag bags are made from recycled truck tarpaulins, seat-belt webbings and bicycle inner-tubes. First designed in 1993 by brothers Markus and Daniel Freitag, the bags bring new life to old materials, keeping over 390 tons of refuse annually out of landfill. All the bags have a lifetime guarantee.

INA

19 (men) and 21 (women) Prince Street, Nolita 10012
212-334-2210 (men)/212-334-9048 (women)
inamen@inanyc.com/inaNolita@inanyc.com
www.inanyc.com
Mon-Sat 12:00-20:00; Sun 12:00-19:00
Subway 6 to Spring Street, or J, Z to Bowery

INA is a very well-edited consignment operation selling current, relevant fashion, with several locations throughout Manhattan, including a dedicated menswear shop in Nolita. The look is upscale contemporary, with shirts and stylish trousers by the likes of Steven Alan and Burberry. There's an excellent selection of designer denims, leather jackets, boots, bags and trilby hats for the cleaned-up downtown hipster. Next door, the women's store offers pretty tops and a great selection of edgy LBDs – think young designer looks such as Leger, Alaïa, Marni, McQueen, Thakoon, Wang, Miu Miu and Marant. Of course there are also Manolos, Louboutins, Jimmy Choos, and a range of accessories to go-with.

Other locations:
15 Bleecker Street, 10012 (men and women) (212-228-8511)

101 Thompson Street, 10012 (women) (212-941-4757)

207 West 18th Street, 10011 (men and women) (212-334-6572)

208 East 73rd Street, 10021 (women) (212-249-0014)

MARMALADE VINTAGE

174 Mott Street, Nolita 10012
212-473-8070
info@marmaladevintage.com
www.marmaladevintage.com
Mon-Sun 13:00-19:00
Subway 6 to Spring Street, or J, Z to Bowery

After 12 years on Ludlow Street in the Lower East Side, compulsive treasure hunter Hannah Kurland put down roots with this shop full of flirty looks for material girls. Kurland has an eye for statement pieces, graphic and ethnic patterns, and geometric shapes; her collection features iconic designers of the 70s, 80s and 90s such as Zandra Rhodes, Norma Kamali, Mary McFadden, Claude Montana, Betsey Johnson, and Giorgio di Sant'Angelo, along with Miyake and Comme des Garçons. "I just buy what I like, with attention to what's trending," Kurland explains. Her shop is "a great place to observe what our customers are wearing" as a harbinger of fashion trends.

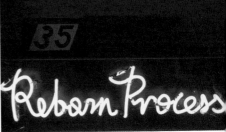

THE QUALITY MENDING CO.

💲💲💲

15 Prince Street, Nolita 10012
212-354-5334
www.thequalitymendingco.com
Mon-Sat 12:00-20:00; Sun 12:00-19:00
Subway N, R to Prince Street, or B, D, F, M to
Broadway-Lafayette

With an Americana ambience reminiscent
of an old general store, this beautifully
curated men's shop was previously known
as Eleven. It features vintage workwear,
khakis, wool trousers and waistcoats,
haberdashery and shoes, and soft home
accessories, along with current American-
made designer denims. Standouts include
Japanese Yukata robes, Belstaff jackets,
and patchworked flannel blankets. The
varsity letter jackets, camp T-shirts
and short-sleeve madras shirts are very
1950s prepster. Owner Oliver Harkness
is a vintage veteran, having started in
London's Camden Market.

REBORN PROCESS

💲💲💲

35 Crosby Street, SoHo 10013
212-226-6306
info@rebornprocess.com
www.rebornprocess.com
Mon-Wed 12:00-19:00;
Thu-Sat 11:00 19:00; Sun 12:00-18:00
Subway 6 to Spring Street,
or 6, N, R, Q, J to Canal Street

This charming little basement shop
features restored and repurposed vintage
clothing displayed amongst old luggage
cases, an antique sewing machine, a cozy
couch, and old books. Developed by a
team of three – a stylist, a model, and a
photographer – the line includes pretty
dresses and blouses, old flannel shirts
updated with zippers and epaulettes, and
decorated Converse trainers, along with
vintage shoes, bags and buttons. While
some items are one-offs, the success of
the collection since its inception in 2010
may result in the development of a
wholesale line.

$ $ $ $ $

RESURRECTION

217 Mott Street, Nolita 10012
212-625-1374
resurrectionnyc@earthlink.net
www.resurrectionvintage.com
Mon-Sat 11:00-19:00; Sun 12:00-19:00
Subway 6 to Spring Street, or J, Z to Bowery

Founded in 1996 by Mark Haddawy and Katy Rodriguez, the New York branch of this Los Angeles boutique carries modern vintage from the 1960s, 70s and 80s that will have you referencing Swinging London, Warhol and *Boogie Nights*. Its boudoir-red, plush interior houses "names you must know" for connoisseurs of Gucci, Pucci, Halston and YSL, and less ubiquitous looks from offbeat designers such as Norma Kamali, Ossie Clark, Zandra Rhodes and Stephen Sprouse. This is serious vintage with price tags to match, including accessories, eyewear and some major jewelry; but if you are not a celebrity, designer, or costume researcher, you could always wait for the shop's highly-anticipated annual July/August sale.

$ $ $

RITUAL VINTAGE

377 Broome Street, Nolita 10013
212-966-4142
info@ritualvintage.com
www.ritualvintage.com
Mon-Sun 12:00-20:00
Subway 6 to Spring Street,
or J, M, Z to Bowery

Formerly known as Exquisite Costume, there is a real respect for history in Stacy Iannacone's collection of vintage clothing, which includes carefully chosen and repaired pieces from the Victorian age, as well as beautiful dresses from the 1920s and 30s and designer pieces from the 60s and 70s. The intimate shop is housed in a former carriage house, where we found a Victorian Dolman, a 1920s blouse in embroidered lawn, a 1930s silk crêpe dress with diamante deco clips, and an iconic Bonnie Cashin pleated heather jersey dress; along with delicate silk slips in powdery skintones and exquisite linen camisoles from the turn of the century. More than vintage, these are quality costumes with historical significance. Designers and celebrities flock here, along with costumers from movies and television. A larger archives is housed in Stacy's showroom at nearby 50 Eldridge Street; by appointment only.

RITUAL VINTAGE:
A PASSION FOR
HISTORICAL CLOTHING

"I have the most awesome job in the world."

Stacy Iannacone, Ritual Vintage

Stacy Iannacone has a passion for historical clothing, fabrics, folk art, hand-worked details, and unique and unusual items. Growing up in Vermont, which she calls "a deeply magical place," she studied photography at Rhode Island School of Design. "I'm mostly self-taught about fashion history," she says. Everything in her shop is hand-selected, and she's a dab hand with a needle and thread, restoring her finds with tender loving care. "I have the most awesome job in the world," she muses. "I travel all over the country."

Stacy clearly values authenticity in her work, and recently furnished a number of pieces for HBO's production of *Boardwalk Empire*. She described it as "The 1920s as it has never been done before, with true authenticity and attention to detail." Despite working with celebrities, musicians, stylists, and photographers, she seems at home in her delightful shop, open since 2006.

WHAT GOES AROUND COMES AROUND

Ⓢ Ⓢ Ⓢ Ⓢ

351 West Broadway, SoHo 10013
212-343-1225
soho@whatgoesaroundnyc.com
www.whatgoesaroundnyc.com
Mon-Sat 11:00-20:00; Sun 12:00-19:00
Subway C, E to Spring Street,
or N, R to Prince Street

What began as a SoHo vintage boutique some 19 years ago has blossomed into one of the best-known vintage businesses in the US, with a store in Los Angeles and recent pop-up shop in Williamsburg, Brooklyn; as well as a by-appointment archive in New Jersey which houses an extensive treasury of vintage clothing and textiles. Co-founders Gerard Maione and Seth Weissner's collection includes women's clothing from the Victorian, Edwardian and Art Deco eras, through 1960s fashion and iconic designer pieces. Their menswear line specializes in denim, military apparel, workwear and footwear. The shop offers pristine vintage mixed with contemporary brands, along with handcrafted 'Custom Vintage' that has been refurbished and recycled.

Other location:
184 Kent Avenue, Williamsburg, Brooklyn 11211

A. TUREN

Ⓢ Ⓢ Ⓢ Ⓢ Ⓢ

85 Stanton Street, Lower East Side 10002
212-533-8200
info@aturennyc.com
www.aturennyc.com
Tues-Sat 12:00-20:00; Sun 12:00-19:00
Subway F, J, M, Z to Delancey & Essex Streets

Ashley Turen customizes and repurposes vintage pieces and customer favorites using hand-painting or glittering, lace, appliqués, buttons or jewelry; turning recycled jeans, cut-off denims, vintage jackets, and even Chanel bags into rock-star one-offs. "I take clothes that might otherwise be trashed, and make them 'in' again," she says. The tiny, modern boutique also carries contemporary designer denim along with pricey T-shirt and jewelry labels.

$$$

ANY OLD IRON

149 Orchard Street, Lower East Side 10002
212-254-4404
andrew@anyoldiron.net
www.anyoldiron.net
Sun-Wed 12:00-19:00;
Thu-Sat 12:00-20:00
Subway F, J, M, Z to Delancey & Essex Streets

At Any Old Iron you will find a unique assortment of men's clothing from the UK, including contemporary pieces, one-offs and reworked vintage; along with antiques and vintage 'bits and bobs' from England such as watch chains, Union Jacks and foppish hats. The store's moniker comes from the cry of the old horse-and-cart scrap collectors, and also refers to an English music hall song about dandyism. The black interior underlines a cheeky, rock-and-roll ambience, and items such as Red Mutha's recycled, customized jackets are not for the bashful.

$$$

ASSEMBLY NEW YORK

170 Ludlow Street, Lower East Side 10002
212-253-5393
www.assemblynewyork.com
Mon-Sun 12:00-21:00
Subway F, J, M, Z to Delancey & Essex Streets

This whitewashed, light-filled space is more SoHo boutique than secondhand shop; while it started with a collection of vintage shoes for men, it now houses curated vintage and new designer merchandise for both men and women, along with charming *objets d'art*. The store is a bit of an artisan's hub, with an ambience of collaboration and design exclusivity. Owner Greg Armas has recently developed a hand-sewn collection of unisex designs "made from natural and historic fabrics in a spirit of a future-primitive instinct". Men's shoes from the 1940s through the 70s are outstanding, as are 1980s pieces from Issey Miyake and Yohji Yamamoto.

$$$

DAVID OWENS VINTAGE CLOTHING

154 Orchard Street, Lower East Side 10002
212-677-3301
Mon-Sun 12:00-20:00
Subway F, J, M, Z to Delancey & Essex Streets

Shoppers rave about the selection, service and reasonable prices at David Owens Vintage Clothing. Beyond the well-curated pre-owned furs, vintage neckties and designer wear, Owens clearly has a flair for the iconic styles, prints and patterns of the 1940s through the 1960s. We found delicate tea dresses of silk or embroidered voile, fur-trimmed cardies, and printed Hawaiian shirts. Standouts included a Gernreich swimsuit and Pucci tunic from the 60s, vintage Hermès ties and scarves, and a more contemporary Bob Mackie gown. The selection of vintage menswear is one of the best in New York, including ties, tiebars and cufflinks from the 40s, and a good assortment of braces, waistcoats, boots and WWII leather outerwear.

MOSCOT

⑤⑤⑤

118 Orchard Street, Lower East Side 10002
212-477-3796
www.moscot.com
Mon-Fri 10:00-19:00; Sat 10:30-18:00;
Sun 12:00-18:00
Subway F, J, M, Z to Delancey & Essex Streets

Sol Moscot Opticians is a New York
institution which began with the 1899
arrival of family patriarch Hyman Moscot
from eastern Europe; he sold eyeglasses
from a pushcart along Orchard Street.
Four generations later, while Moscot's
medical and technical services are fully
modernized, the store maintains its
vintage ambiance and a great selection of
reproduction eyewear whose fans include
Johnny Depp, Daniel Day-Lewis, Alicia
Keys and Cee Lo Green – and most New
Yorkers. The Moscot brand of vintage-
inspired eyewear is distributed globally,
but its Orchard Street home supplies
authentic atmosphere and service; and
there is still a Dr Moscot.

THE REFORMATION

⑤⑤⑤

156 Ludlow Street, Lower East Side 10002
646-448-4925
alex@thereformation.com
www.thereformation.com
Mon-Sat 12:00-20:00; Sun 12:00-19:00
Subway F, J, M, Z to Delancey & Essex Streets

Much more than just a vintage shop, this
"new approach to fashion" is a brand
of vintage and repurposed clothing
originating in Los Angeles. While not
for bargain hunters, the limited editions
and one-offs combine designer style with
the brand's intention that 80 percent of
all their materials are reclaimed. The
line comprises standard vintage, curated
statement pieces, and refashioned
clothing made from reclaimed vintage
garments and dead stock fabric. Women's
vintage and repurposed knitwear,
separates, dresses, outerwear, and
accessories are offered, along with a
small but growing line of men's shirts and
sweaters; the shop also features select
contemporary brands. In a new space
since October 2011, designer/owner Yael
Aflalo has created a luxurious and cozy
atmosphere with Turkish carpets and a
four-poster bed.

$ $ $

SOME ODD RUBIES

151 Ludlow Street, Lower East Side 10002
212-353-1736
info@someoddrubies.com
www.someoddrubies.com
Mon-Fri 13:00-20:00; Sat 12:00-20:00;
Sun 12:00-19:00
Subway F, J, M, Z to Delancey & Essex Streets

A little pink jewelbox of a shop, Some
Odd Rubies offers a mix of one-off,
reconstructed vintage pieces and a
limited collection of new styles made
from dead stock fabrics. Designers/
partners Ruby Canner, Summer Phoenix
and Odessa Whitmire have a keen eye for
silky fabrics and pretty floral prints, and
the emphasis is on wearable, feminine
dresses. The partners research vintage
finds from all over, then nip and tuck to
change the silhouette and make them
flattering for modern bodies. They'll help
you accessorize, too, with a mix of vintage
and new jewelry, and the oversized
boudoir-style dressing room makes it a
pleasure to play dress-up.

MOSCOT: SHOPPING IN SOL MOSCOT'S WITH A REAL NEW YORKER

Edward Capolongo has lived in New York since the 1970s, originally on Jane Street, which is downtown in Greenwich Village; and he's a long-time customer of Moscot's. The neighborhood was an Irish/Italian/Jewish mix back then. He's now moved to Brooklyn because the neighborhood became too gentrified. "I moved out when peppers hit $1.50 each."

"I've always felt comfortable coming to Moscot's," Edward maintains. "I used to bring Dr. Joel a box of figs; we'd barter eyeglasses for vegetables." Dr. Joel, the grandson of founder Hyman Moscot, was always tan from his visits to Florida. "You'd look this way too if you spent a month in God's little waiting room," he would joke.

ⓈⓈⓈⓈ
EPONYMY

466 Bergen Street, Park Slope 11217
718-789-0301
hello@shopeponymy.com
www.shopeponymy.com
Tues-Fri 12:00-19:00; Sat 11:00-19:00;
Sun 12:00-18:00
Subway F, G to Bergen Street

Antique mirrors and works of art line the walls of this luxurious women's boutique, hung with chandeliers and furnished with period cabinetry displaying Andrea Miller's charming vintage and contemporary wares. This gracious Brooklyn outpost is a surprising mix of clothing store, gallery, and antique shop; the vintage clothing and jewelry from the turn of the century through the 1960s mingles with carefully chosen modern brands.

ⓈⓈⓈⓈ
EVA GENTRY CONSIGNMENT

371 Atlantic Avenue, Boerum Hill 11217
718-522-3522
consignment@evagentry.com
www.evagentry.com
Mon-Sat 12:00-19:00; Sun 12:00-18:00
Subway A, C, G to Hoyt-Schermerhorn Streets

This haven for gently-used or unsold designer clothing, shoes and accessories for women is a cut above Brooklyn's generally funky vintage thrift shops. Carefully selected and gently (or never) worn, the fashion editor-worthy merchandise is arranged by color, and sold on consignment for about 40 percent of its high-end, designer-level retail value. Labels range from Alaïa to Zero + Maria Cornejo, and may include clearance items from Butter, the owner's nearby boutique. All unsold consignment merchandise is donated to CAMBA, a group of women's rehabilitation and homeless shelters in Brooklyn.

GUVNOR'S VINTAGE THRIFT

$$

178 Fifth Avenue, Park Slope 11217
718-230-4887
info@guvnorsnyc.com
www.guvnorsnyc.com
Sun-Wed 12:00-19:30;
Thu/Fri 12:00-20:00; Sat 11:00-20:00
Subway R to Union Street

Part vintage, part thrift, Guvnor's has a
rockabilly vibe based on owner Suzette
Sundae's penchant for rock-and-roll
clothing from the 1950s through the 1980s.
Be prepared for some sensory overload
as you browse (to the sound of vintage
rock) through jumpsuits and motorcycle
boots, maxi dresses and embroidered felt
vests, sequined evening gowns and batik'd
beachwear. While some pieces may be
a bit scruffy, they've all got attitude, and
you can't beat the prices. Guvnor's also
buys, sells and trades on consignment,
and a 'minister of alterations' will provide
tailoring to fit if necessary.

ODD TWIN

$$

164 Fifth Avenue, Park Slope 11217
718-633-8946
www.oddtwin.com
Mon-Fri 12:00-20:00; Sat/Sun 11:00-20:00
Subway R to Union Street

Well-edited and well-priced women's and
men's vintage clothing from the 1920s
through the 1980s mixes with jewelry,
accessories, and a selection of vintage
home items at Odd Twin. The pretty
frocks from the 1950s, go-go dresses
from the 60s, and hard-rock looks from
the 80s will appeal to party-goers, and
the vintage baby clothes are nothing
short of adorable. Owner Francesca
Neville's passion for vintage collecting
shines through in her Born Again line of
refurbished and remodeled dresses.

OLAF'S MEN'S VINTAGE

$$

453 Court Street, Carroll Gardens 11231
347-457-5796
olafsmensvintage@blogspot.com
Mon-Fri 12:00-20:00; Sat 11:00-21:00;
Sun 11:00-18:00
Subway F, G to Carroll Street

Opened by the owners of Olive's Very
Vintage, this men's shop is dedicated to a
rugged American aesthetic of Adirondack
camps and natural fibres. Think flannel
shirts, 1950s button-downs, skinny ties,
tweed hunting jackets and wing-tips
from the likes of L.L. Bean and Pendleton,
cozied up to camp blankets and patchwork
quilts, camping equipment (canteens,
binoculars) and manly furnishings.

OLIVE'S VERY VINTAGE

$$$$

434 Court Street, Carroll Gardens 11231
718-243-9094
info@olivesveryvintage.com
www.olivesveryvintage.com
Mon-Fri 12:00-20:00; Sat 11:00-20:00;
Sun 10:00-18:00
Subway F, G to Carroll Street

Fashion stylist and vintage collector
Jen McCulloch opened Olive's in 2001;
the shop has become one of the city's
favorites, attracting stylists and design
teams who are inspired by the vintage
clothing and accessories from the late
1800s through the 1980s. Many of the
pieces are perfect for parties and special
occasions and include designer vintage
from the likes of Oscar de la Renta, Norma
Kamali, Bob Mackie and Hattie Carnegie.
There are pretty shoes, sparkly jewelry
and accessories, as well as old *Vogue*
sewing patterns, fabrics and trims.

PONY

69 Fifth Avenue, Park Slope 11217
718-622-7669
info@ponyshopnyc.com
www.ponyshopnyc.com
Mon-Sat 12:00-20:00; Sun 12:00-19:00

Brand new in 2011, Pony buys, sells, and swaps cute, freshly-laundered secondhand women's clothing at an affordable level. Brands such as Club Monaco, Marc by Marc Jacobs, and Tracy Reese are sorted by color and helpfully tagged with information about the brand and the fabric. While there are a few vintage pieces mixed in, most of the merchandise is gently-worn contemporary.

SMITH + BUTLER

225 Smith Street, Carroll Gardens 11231
917-855-4295
shop@smithbutler.com
www.smithbutler.com
Mon 12:00-19:00; Tues/Wed 12:00-19:30;
Thu-Sat 11:00-19:30; Sun 12:00-18:00
Subway F, G to Bergen Street or Carroll Street

Housed in a beautiful 1890s building that reflects Brooklyn's old-world culture, Smith + Butler was established in 2008. A mix of modern utilitarian menswear brands, hand-crafted jewelry, secondhand accessories, antique furniture and homewares, vintage motorcycles and biker paraphernalia creates an authentic atmosphere. Secondhand men's shoes and boots, Amish leathercraft, vintage camp blankets and old Levi's reflect the trending of all-American classics. Owner Marylynn Piotrowski says her goal is to "give visitors a sense of old New York, and the people who now live here."

⑤⑤⑤

ABOUT GLAMOUR

107A North Third Street, Williamsburg 11249
718-599-3044
www.aboutglamour.net
Sun-Thu 12:00-20:00; Fri 12:00-21:00;
Sat 12:00-22:00
Subway L to Bedford Avenue

Part boutique, part art gallery, About
Glamour's presentation of European and
Japanese vintage clothing for men and
women, tea sets and glassware, and quirky
Japanese cards, postcards and wrapping
papers reflects a finely-honed design
ethic. The well-edited mix of old and new
includes silk scarves, French tees, and
reasonably priced secondhand fashion
from the likes of Agnes B, Vivienne
Westwood, Yohji Yamamoto, and Comme
des Garçons; along with dead stock
hosiery and footwear; Japanese pocket
squares, bow ties, socks and umbrellas;
and some repurposed fashion. The 2400
square-foot former warehouse also houses
the AG Gallery, showcasing local artists.
Hours may vary, so call first.

⑤⑤⑤⑤

AMARCORD VINTAGE FASHION

223 Bedford Avenue, Williamsburg 11211
718-963-4001
us@amarcoredvintagefashion.com
www.amarcordvintagefashion.com
Mon-Sun 12:00-20:00
Subway L to Bedford Avenue

Bright, pretty, and a fashionista's dream,
Amarcord Vintage Fashion is consistently
top-rated for its collection of primarily
European designer vintage clothing
from the 1940s to the 1980s, much of it
pristine dead stock. Owners Patti Bordoni
and Marco Liotta opened their first
shop in New York's East Village in 2000,
and the Williamsburg shop followed in
2002. Fashion is the key word here, and
Amarcord offers both men and women
a selection of well-curated, beautifully
merchandised, top-quality vintage
clothing and accessories that is seasonally
updated and on-trend. Visiting in summer,
we found classic country club sportswear,
accessorized with pretty straw bags
and resin jewelry from the 50s and 60s.
Nearby is Amarcord's by-appointment-
only archive showroom, a favorite of
media and fashion industry professionals,
with more than 50,000 unique pieces
of vintage clothing and accessories
for rent. Amarcord offers vintage in its
truest sense: "Having an excellence that
survives the passing of time." Expect to
pay accordingly.

Other locations:
252 Lafayette Street, Nolita 10012
(212-431-4161)

Showroom and Archives, 22 Conselyea
Street, Williamsburg 11211 (718-388-2884)
(by appointment only)

$ $

BEACON'S CLOSET

88 North 11th Street, Williamsburg 11249
718-486-0816
service@beaconscloset.com
www.beaconscloset.com
Mon-Fri 11:00-21:00; Sat/Sun 11:00-20:00
Subway L to Bedford Avenue

Beacon's Closet is a buyer and reseller of secondhand and 'modern vintage' clothing and accessories with unbeatable prices. The 5500 square-foot Williamsburg store is the original and largest of three shops, where neighborhood fashionistas bring their unwanted items for cash or store credit. Items not chosen for resale are donated to charity, as is a portion of the store's profits. The store is merchandised by category and by color; there are labels such as Cynthia Rowley, Tahari, Calypso, Badgley Mischka, and Sitbon, along with high-street retail brands. Men's fashion includes polo shirts from Nike Golf and Marc Jacobs, and smart dress shirts from the likes of Barneys New York, Hugo Boss, and Etro; there's also a small selection of men's suits. There are sweaters, trousers, hats, shoes, handbags, belts, jewelry, and sunglasses galore.

Other locations:
10 West 13th Street, Greenwich Village 10011 (917-261-4863)

92 Fifth Avenue, Park Slope 11217 (718-230-1630)

💲💲💲

MALIN LANDAEUS

155 North Sixth Street, Williamsburg 11211
646-361-0261
malin@landaeus.com
www.malinlandaeus.tumblr.com
Sun-Thu 11:00-21:00, Fri/Sat 11:00-22:30
Subway L to Bedford Avenue

In business for six years, this pretty shop full of 1980s-90s feminine fashion emerged from a booth at nearby weekend market Artists & Fleas and has become a go-to source for the city's fashion designers, stylists and photographers. With a nearby archival showroom (by appointment only), Swedish-born Landaeus has the eye of a stylist, and both the clothing and the merchandising (by color), given a new theme each season, are impeccable. Appropriately priced pieces range from classic skirts and silk blouses to printed day dresses in flowing rayon crêpe, along with iconic 80s fashion from designers such as Norma Kamali and Betsey Johnson. An amazing assortment of hats, scarves, belts, jewelry, and shoes includes a collection of the well-made oxfords, boots and booties of Joan & David and Bandolino from the 1980s. Malin and her daughter Nova will help style your look, serve you tea and homemade organic cake, and quickly become your best friends. "You can come here and feel that you are taken care of," she promises.

💲💲💲

LE GRAND STRIP (FILLE DE JOIE)

197 Grand Street, Williamsburg 11211
718-599-3525
cc@legrandstrip.com
www.legrandstrip.com
Mon-Sat 12:00-20:00 (may open later on Fridays in summer); Sun 12:00-19:00
Subway L to Bedford Avenue

With its saucy name it's no surprise to find this vintage boutique full of cheeky, sexy pieces culled from Paris and the French Riviera, along with American fashion from the 80s and lots of pretty lingerie. French owner C.C. McGurr has an eye for rhinestones, sequins, fringe, poufs and prom dresses, as well as the silk caftans and peasant blouses worn by the Saint-Tropez chic. Accessories are also *très jolie*, with flirty hats, jewelry and vintage shoes from Christian Dior, Charles Jourdan and Sonia Rykiel, to name a few. Silk corsets and trousseau nightwear, along with chemises and petticoats worked in *broderie anglais* from the Marché aux Puces, Paris, are utterly charming. With its crystal chandelier, boudoir lamps, oriental rugs, curvy red couches, and brass bed strewn with pillows, hatboxes and scarves, Le Grand Strip makes shopping a sensory experience.

$ $

VICE VERSA

241 Bedford Avenue, Williamsburg 11211
718-782-8847
www.viceversavintage.com
Mon-Thu 13:00-20:00; Fri/Sat 12:00-22:00;
Sun 12:00-20:00
Subway L to Bedford Avenue

Every inch of rack, wall and shelf space at Vice Versa is tightly packed with bargain-priced modern vintage and secondhand fashion. While there's the occasional wedding dress or fur jacket, most of the merchandise is casual in attitude: denims, T-shirts, fleece, workwear, cowboy boots, trainers and headwear, with a better selection of menswear than most. The shirt rack includes flannels, madras and patchwork; there is also a nice selection of 70s and 80s dresses, long skirts, knitwear such as crocheted ponchos and granny shawls, and costume jewelry.

Malin Landaeus:
Almond cake and cherry muffins

Malin Landaeus believes in making women feel beautiful. Her Swedish aesthetic embodies a sense of individual style that is not about trend, but is based on "sustainable thinking," celebrating all that is lovely and well-made. She cares for her customers with almond cake, cherry muffins and a Reiki-master's sense of calm.

As a child Malin styled her family as well as her Barbie doll. "I've always had an eye since I was little," she confides. She came to New York in 1987 to study at the Fashion Institute of Technology (FIT); the birth of her daughter, called Nova after the fall of Berlin, inspired her to become an avid environmentalist. She began working with organic cotton products for childrenswear in California; then decided to make a positive impact on the environment by collecting, selling and repurposing vintage clothing. A personal turning point forced her to place her own well-curated closet on sale at the flea market, quickly leading to recognition by the city's fashion professionals, and the establishment of her shop. "The hardest times in life are those of personal growth," she believes.

"THE HARDEST TIMES IN LIFE ARE THOSE OF PERSONAL GROWTH"

MALIN LANDAEUS,
MALIN LANDAEUS

Nova (left) and Malin

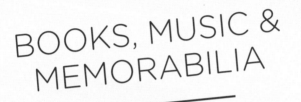

BOOKS, MUSIC & MEMORABILIA

Books / Vinyl / Posters / Musical
Instruments / Mash-ups

AS THE GATEWAY TO A NATION OF IMMIGRANTS, NEW YORK IS THE EPITOME OF MASH-UP CULTURE. NEW YORKERS EMBODY INTELLECTUAL CURIOSITY AND CULTURAL DIVERSITY; SO IT'S NO SURPRISE TO FIND SHOPS FILLED WITH EVERYTHING FROM PRIMITIVE ARTIFACTS TO VICTORIAN CURIOSITIES, INDUSTRIAL IMPLEMENTS, AND MID-CENTURY MODERN COLLECTIBLES; ALONG WITH MEDICAL INSTRUMENTS, KITCHEN UTENSILS, OLD CAMERAS AND ELECTRONICS, BUTTON COLLECTIONS, POSTERS AND CHARTS, AND WACKY BITS AND BOBS OF EVERY KIND. NEW YORK'S COLLECTORS ARE ABLE TO SOURCE MUCH OF THEIR VINTAGE AMERICANA IN THE FARMING COMMUNITIES OF THE NEARBY HUDSON VALLEY, AND CATSKILL AND BERKSHIRE MOUNTAINS, WHERE EARLY DUTCH, ENGLISH AND GERMAN SETTLERS IMPARTED THEIR AESTHETICS TO HANDMADE ITEMS FOR THE HOMESTEAD.

It's also no surprise that in a city with a long-standing and healthy interest in music, theatre and publishing, there's a plethora of secondhand music and bookstores harking back to an era when these merchants flocked together on Book Row (along Fourth Avenue), Tin Pan Alley (West 28th Street, and later on Broadway), and Radio Row (Cortlandt Street). While these enclaves are now dispersed, New York still claims its share of independent shops offering vintage and rare collectibles for the discerning shopper.

$$$

30TH STREET GUITARS

236 West 30th Street, Midtown West 10001
212-868-2660
30thstreetguitars@verzon.net
www.30thstreetguitars.com
Mon-Fri 11:00-18:00 (Thu to 20:00);
Sat 11:00-17:00
Subway 1, 2, 3, A, C, E to 34th Street-Penn
Station, or 1 to 28th Street

Founded by premier luthier and repair
master Matt Brewster in 1997, 30th Street
Guitars specializes in vintage collectible
and secondhand guitars, pedals, and
amps. The emphasis is on electric guitars
and bass from Gibson and Fender; and
Brewster's in-house line of Rust 'relic'
guitars for a more affordable option.
New York's working musicians go here
for repair work and customization.

$$$

ACADEMY RECORDS & CDS

12 West 18th Street, Chelsea 10011
212-242-3000
www.academy-records.com
Sun-Wed 11:00-19:00; Thu-Sat 11:00-20:00
Subway 4, 5, 6, N, R, Q, L to Union Square,
or F, M to 14th Street or 23rd Street

Much like a used bookshop, Academy
Records has something for everyone, from
rare vinyl to popular CDs. Classical and
jazz aficionados will be delighted with the
opportunity to browse through endless
bins to fill the holes in their collections –
the shop claims to be the largest library
of used classical recordings in the city
– and there are hard-to-find recordings
of Broadway, dance music, comedy, pop,
and country music at reasonable prices.
The staff is knowledgeable and it's easy to
spend hours here. An alternate location in
the East Village focuses on jazz and pop
music, while "the mother ship," Academy
Records Annex in Williamsburg, claims to
warehouse over 25,000 titles.

Other locations:
415 East 12th Street, 10009 (212-780-9166)

96 North Sixth Street, Williamsburg,
Brooklyn 11249 (718-218-8200)

$$$$$

CHELSEA GUITARS

224 West 23rd Street, Chelsea 10001
212-675-4993
chelseaguitars@gmail.com
www.chelseaguitars.com
Mon-Sun 11:00-19:00
Subway 1, F, M, C, E to 23rd Street

Tucked away in a street-level shop under
the infamous Chelsea Hotel, Dan's
Chelsea Guitars is Mecca for visiting rock-
and-roll royalty as well as for local artists
and passionate beginners. Established
in 1988, the shop manages to hang on to
the neighborhood's essential funkiness
in the midst of Chelsea's gentrification.
A faux T-Rex head crashing through the
ceiling is your first clue that the staff and
customers alike take themselves none too
seriously while browsing, playing and just
hanging out. Vintage electric guitars from
the 40s and 50s include Gibson Les Pauls;
and there are Martin or Gibson acoustics,
Fender bass, and other selections ranging
into the 1980s. You can also pick out a
decent beginner's instrument with the
advice of the knowledgeable staff.
The shop keeps musician's hours,
so call ahead.

$ $ $ $

MANTIQUES MODERN

146 West 22nd Street, Chelsea 10011
212-206-1494
info@mantiquesmodern.com
www.mantiquesmodern.com
Mon-Fri 10:30-18:30; Sat/Sun 11:00-19:00
Subway 1, F, M to 23rd Street

This antiques gallery with a decidedly masculine slant is a wonderland of 20th century industrial and mid-century artifacts, artfully displayed in a spare, concrete-floored gallery. The collection of art, luggage, glass, brass, timepieces, frames, machine bits, scientific instruments, and aids to the enjoyable vices of drinking, smoking and gambling has been brought together by three owners who share an excellent aesthetic. Owner Cory Margolis, whose parents are antique dealers, explained: "The secret to our success is taking hundreds of categories from different decades, and making them work as a homogenized aesthetic under one roof." Prices are on the high-end of retail; Mantiques also sells to select galleries and retail clients in London and New York.

$ $

COLONY RECORDS

1619 Broadway, Midtown West 10019
212-265-2050
www.colonymusic.com
Mon-Sat 09:00-01:00; Sun 10:00-00:00
Subway 1, 2, C, E to 50th Street,
or N, R to 49th Street

Located in the historic Brill Building, which at one time housed 165 music businesses including composers, publishers and studios, Colony Records is a relic of Tin Pan Alley, New York's once-powerful music business. While there's a current selection of wax, CDs and karaoke from Broadway theatre productions as well as from movies, you'll also find standards by the decade and boxed sets from iconic crooners such as Sinatra and Crosby. Colony specializes in current and vintage sheet music and scores, from rock to pop to Broadway musicals. There are retro posters from concerts and the Broadway stage, as well as music memorabilia for the Times Square tourist traffic.

$ $ $ $

PERRY RITTER

71 West 47th Street, suite 704, Midtown West 10036
212-302-5443/212-956-6174
www.perryritter.com
Mon-Fri 06:00-17:00
Subway B, D, F, M to 47th-50th Streets, Rockefeller Center

Perry Ritter repairs, restores and overhauls woodwind and brass instruments – hence the unusual hours – and along the way has amassed a carefully curated array of vintage instruments for sale to serious musicians or collectors, including Selmer Mark VI tenor saxophones from the 1950s and 60s (most horn players will tell you these are the best). The walls of Perry's small studio are hung with some museum-quality instruments, such as a Selmer rosewood contra alto E-flat clarinet, and a gold-plated double-bell euphonium circa 1904. With a passion for his craft, in his spare time Ritter creates charming sculptures from the disassembled bits and pieces of retired instruments.

ROGUE MUSIC

'BIG ED' SULLIVAN

"Everybody who is anybody has bought here," claims 'Big Ed' Sullivan, blues guitarist and owner of Rogue Music. Judging by the number of musicians hanging around the store, it's not an idle boast. Sulllivan hails from Brooklyn and has been a mainstay of the New York blues and rockabilly scene for years. His blues jam session at the Red Lion in Greenwich Village is world famous. "Ed has been around forever and knows his stuff," says fellow musician Mike Merda of City Boys.

"Everybody who is anybody has bought here"

'BIG ED' SULLIVAN, ROGUE MUSIC

$$\$\,\$\,\$$

ROGUE MUSIC

220 West 30th Street, Midtown West 10001
212-629-5073
ed@roguemusic.com
www.roguemusic.com
Mon/Sat 11:00-18:00; Tues-Fri 11:00-20:00
Subway 1, 2, 3, A, C, E to
34th Street-Penn Station

Rogue was the name of a New York band
in the 1980s; when its keyboardist Dick
Michaels needed to sell his instrument,
the Rogue Music store was born. Stocked
with a medley of new, vintage and used
guitars, pedals, studio gear, keyboards,
synthesizers, and drum machines, Rogue
carries "audio stuff" from the 70s and 80s,
with woodwind repair in the basement. All
of the staff are professional musicians. It's
a great place to find secondhand musical
kit; the shared knowledge is priceless.

$$ $$

ARCHANGEL ANTIQUES

334 East Ninth Street, East Village 10003
212-260-9313
archangelantique@gmail.com
www.archangelantiques.com
Wed-Sat 15:00-19:00
Subway L to First Avenue, or 6 to Astor Place

After several years of working auctions, estate sales and antique shows from Maine to Florida, Richard and Gail Busche opened Archangel Antiques in 1993; a few years later they were joined by fellow collector/manager Michael Duggan, and expanded into the shop next door. Their specialty is buttons – Gail estimates as many as two million buttons – dating from the 1850s through the 1970s, including Victorian glass, Deco Bakelite, mother-of-pearl, metal, wood, leather and more. A fine collection of vintage cufflinks and estate jewelry should not be missed (we fell in love with a coral cameo bracelet); and Native American turquoise is well represented. Eyewear, optical instruments and oddities include Civil War-era eyeglasses, opera glasses, compasses, microscopes, and lamps on bases made from musical instruments; along with old luggage, cigarette cases, piggy banks, salt-and-pepper sets, perfume bottles, sewing patterns, yarn, laces and braids – and we haven't even mentioned the vintage clothing. Hours of fun, and prices can be negotiated.

§§ – §§§

BONNIE SLOTNICK COOKBOOKS

163 West Tenth Street,
Greenwich Village 10014
212-989-8962
bonnieslotnickbooks@earthlink.net
www.bonnieslotnickcookbooks.com
Most days 13:00-19:00 (call ahead)
Subway 1 to Christopher Street

Editor and collector Bonnie Slotnick has filled her 350 square-foot shop with some 4000 out-of-print and antique cookbooks, along with vintage kitchen utensils and linens. Here you'll find all-American compilations from Betty Crocker and *Good Housekeeping*, classic cookbooks from the world's most respected chefs, community cookbooks, old restaurant guides, and books on etiquette; along with a veritable world tour of cuisines, organized by country. The collection is constantly changing and evolving, with some items dating from the 19th century; and rare items such as *Mrs. Beeton's Everyday Cookery* sell quickly. To Bonnie, a former cookbook editor, a cookbook is much more than a collection of recipes or its resale value; it can offer the reader a sense of history, world culture, or comfort and nostalgia. "It's about the feel of the book," she says. "If you buy it for the right reason, you won't want to part with it."

💲💲

EAST VILLAGE BOOKS

99 St. Mark's Place, East Village 10009
212-477-8647
findtimmy@yahoo.com
www.buyusedbooksnewyork.com
Mon-Thu 13:00-23:00; Fri 13:00-00:00;
Sat 12:00-23:00; Sun 13:00-21:00
Subway L to First Avenue, or 6 to Astor Place

Called by many "the best used bookstore in NYC," East Village Books buys its eclectic stock from estate sales and scholarly collections. While the basement location makes it seem a bit of a dungeon, books are organized by sections such as art, music, fashion, occult and mysticism, nature, classic fiction, philosophy and theory, travel, media studies – and yes, comics and anti-establishment. In residence on funky St. Mark's Place for 18 years, it's truly the intellectual's used bookstore, and pleasingly cheap. Call first if you are planning to visit early or late.

EAST VILLAGE MUSIC STORE

21 East Third Street, East Village 10003
212-991-4930
zippy@broadviewnet.net
www.evmnyc.com
Mon-Fri 12:00-20:00; Sat 14:00-20:00
Subway 6 to Astor Place,
or F, M to Second Avenue

This low-key, concrete-floored shop offers everything for the musician in a small space with a surprisingly large selection of new, used and vintage musical instruments. Guitars, banjos, violins, keyboards, audio equipment, soundboards, percussion and wind instruments are bought, sold, traded, rented and repaired here, all at reasonable prices. While the staff is knowledgeable, hours can be erratic, so call first if you plan to visit early in the day.

$$$ - $$$$

KABINETT & KAMMER

174 East Second Street, East Village 10009
646-476-5565
www.kabinettandkammer.com
Wed-Sat 12:00-20:00; Sun 12:00-17:00
Subway F, M to Second Avenue,
or F, J, M, Z to Delancey & Essex Street

This modern curiosity shop full of medical, zoological and botanical ephemera and utilitarian mid-19th century furniture is the work of Sean Scherer and Rick Gilbert, and an offshoot of their gallery in bucolic Andes, New York, in the Catskill Mountains. As designers and collectors with a following among New York's creative community, the two have brought their unique aesthetic to this small shop, with its tin ceiling and walls papered in old medical texts. Museum-quality collectibles include vintage medical charts from the Czech Republic and Germany, botanical prints, and school charts. There are apothecary items, specimens under bell jars, beautiful sea shells, and a vintage crocodile skull, not to mention a taxidermy menagerie; displayed alongside items such as an antique milking stool, a giant copper pot, and old sports equipment. With a nod to the naturalists and collectors of the Victorian age, Kabinett & Kammer's oddities provide thought-provoking contrast to contemporary interior design.

$$$ - $$$$
SPIRIT AND MATTER

180 East Tenth Street, East Village 10009
917-881-7349
Mon-Sun 15:00-19:00
Subway L to First Avenue, or 6 to Astor Place

This wonderfully quirky collection of antique indigenous artifacts and handiwork evokes travel to "the dark past and the bright future," according to owner Rick Gallagher, who grew up in the UK with "a love of the macabre." The cozy shop, furnished with 1930s furniture and vintage rugs, houses carved ivory jewelry, shell art, fetishes, and beads from the South Pacific, South America, Africa and Native American peoples. They're mixed with old weapons, tools, oars and paddles, locks and keys, antique paint sets, art papers, and rubber stamps. Worth the visit, it's a good idea to call ahead to confirm opening hours.

$ $ $

STRAND BOOK STORE

828 Broadway, Greenwich Village 10003
212-473-1452
www.strandbooks.com
Mon-Sat 09:30-22:30; Sun 11:00-22:30
Subway 4, 5, 6, L, N, R, Q
to 14th Street-Union Square

The independent Strand Book Store is a
New York institution and the sole survivor
of the city's Book Row, once home to 48
bookstores. Established in 1927 by Ben
Bass and named after London's famous
publishing street, the store remains in
the family, comprising more than 2.5
million new, used and rare books housed
in 40,000 square feet over three floors.
The rare book room, on the third floor,
specializes in early editions, art books,
prints, maps, classic games and ephemera;
while the second floor features art and
architecture, fashion, design, comics, and
a lively children's department. The rare
book room closes daily at 6:15 p.m. but
often hosts events such as readings, book
signings and author chats.

$$$

FOUNTAIN PEN HOSPITAL

10 Warren Street, Tribeca 10007
212-964-0580
info@fountainpenhospital.com
www.fountainpenhospital.com
Mon-Fri 07:30-17:30
Subway 1, 2, 3, A, C to Chambers Street

A fine selection of new, vintage and limited edition pens are proudly exhibited – for sale – at this family-owned gallery and repair shop, founded in 1946 and still owned and run by the Wiederlight family. Vintage models include Mont Blancs, Watermans, Sheaffer, Goldfinks, Pelikans, and a large selection of unused vintage Parkers and Parker 51 Vacumatics. With their gold-filled, marbleized, mahogany or etched barrels, many are true collectibles.

$⑤ $⑤

HOUSING WORKS, BOOKSTORE CAFÉ

126 Crosby Street, SoHo 10012
212-334-3324
info@housingworks.org
www.housingworks.org
Mon-Fri 10:00-21:00; Sat/Sun 10:00-17:00
Subway N, R to Prince Street,
or B, D, F, M to Broadway-Lafayette

This wonderful old space with its wooden balcony, endless shelves of books and aroma of popcorn is what you'd wish your local library to be, with Friday night happy hours, storytimes and singalongs for kids, and a yearly open-air street fair. The bookstore is part of the Housing Works organization, which operates a dozen volunteer-run thrift shops (see p110) around New York whose proceeds benefit the city's victims of AIDS, HIV and homelessness. The space is a treasure-trove of secondhand books and CDs, including collectibles: we found first editions by Stephen King, Scott Turow, Peter Matthiessen and Saul Bellow. With more donations than they can shelve, the bookstore also sells 'books by the foot': decorative assortments of art books, contemporary fiction, Victorian era and the like. A great venue, cool events and a worthy cause make this much more than a secondhand bookstore.

$ $ $

THE MYSTERIOUS BOOKSHOP

58 Warren Street, Tribeca 10007
212-587-1011
info@mysteriousbookshop.com
www.mysteriousbookshop.com
Mon-Sat 11:00-19:00
Subway 1, 2, 3, A, C to Chambers Street

Thrills and chills await mystery fans at Tribeca's Mysterious Bookshop, the country's largest assemblage of new and secondhand suspense, espionage, crime and detective fiction, including collectible limited editions, and rare and signed first editions. This quiet, library-like shop furnished with leather armchairs and sofas features a wall of Sherlock Holmes novels, as well as vintage Haycraft-Queen Cornerstone and Queen's Quorum titles. Celebrating its 34th anniversary this year, the bookshop was founded by Otto Penzler, well-known publisher, editor and writer of mystery genre.

💲💲💲

PHILIP WILLIAMS POSTERS

122 Chambers Street, Tribeca 10007
212-513-0313
postermuseum@gmail.com
www.postermuseum.com
Mon-Sat 11:00-19:00
(Mon in July/Aug closed)
Subway 1, 2, 3, A, C to Chambers Street

Part retail establishment, part museum, Philip Williams claims his poster collection is the largest in the world. The 12,600 square-foot space fills three floors and is stacked high with posters from around the world. Philip explains that with the advent of color lithography in France during the late 19th century, artists often made posters to make ends meet; these were collected as art by the French middle class and have survived through the century. He began collecting 40 years ago: "I saw a big disconnect between the prices and values of posters – they are still inexpensive relative to their true value." The shop also houses early film posters from the silent era, collections of sheet music from the 1920s and 30s, archival issues of American *Life* magazines, and folk art from the American south.

⑤⑤⑤
WORKING CLASS

168 Duane Street, Tribeca 10013
212-941-1199
info@workingclassinc.com
www.workingclassinc.com
Mon-Sun 11:00-19:00
Subway 1, 2, 3, A, C to Chambers Street

Downtown Manhattan might be the last place you would expect to find an old-fashioned general store. David Metcalf and Rhea O'Brien launched their dry goods emporium above their basement-level advertising business in the mid-90s, when Tribeca was starting to boom. "When we bought the space for the advertising business we thought it would be great to have a company store instead of a reception area," Rhea explains. The shop contains an eclectic assortment of antiques, reproductions, collectibles, furniture, clothing and accessories designed to appeal to admirers of Victoriana and the industrial revolution. A Yorkshire native, David travels back to the UK several times a year, returning with "suitcases full" of silver and plate, coronation china, teapots, vintage tins, enamel ware, Whitby jet brooches, perfume bottles, and the like. Nothing pricey or posh here – it's strictly working class.

§ § §

WRK DESIGN

32 Prince Street, Nolita 10012
212-947-2281
showroom@wrkdesign.com
www.wrkdesign.com
Mon-Sun 11:00-19:00
Subway N, R to Prince Street,
or 6 to Spring Street

WRK is an interior design and building business that has recently opened a showroom featuring found objects that reflect America's early industrial history. Partners Josh Farley and Jeremy Floto describe themselves as "designers, builders, scavengers and treasure hunters." They find, fix and transform objects from abandoned factories, storage depots, dumpsters and flea markets, using them in their creative interiors for shops, restaurants, and lucky home owners. Housed in an old school along Prince Street, the showroom is a quirky assortment of old industrial pieces and antiques: ladders, lockers, metal baskets, tool caddies, chairs, stools, tables, locks and keys, photos, toys, ledgers, type, bobbins, linens and rugs. Farley and Floto have captured an American aesthetic that speaks to authenticity and work ethic; it's a look we noticed in a growing number of downtown shops.

$

BROWNSTONE TREASURES

220 Court Street, Cobble Hill 11201
718-237-1838
www.brownstonetreasures.com
Tues-Sun 11:00-18:00
Subway F, G to Bergen Street

A bit shabby, a bit chic, this attractively cluttered shop offers vintage furniture, clothing, jewelry, and life's little necessities from the 20th century. Furniture ranges from country cupboards and wardrobes to Danish modern and kitchen tables. We found a fold-out wooden sewing basket as well as an electric Singer in its oak cabinet, both reminiscent of mom's in the 1950s; along with a set of leather jewelry drawers. There's an excellent assortment of brooches and clip-on earrings, wide ties and chain belts from the 70s, old nylon slips and nighties, retro Berkshire hosiery in the original boxes, buttons and sewing notions, old 45 records and vintage photos, and a small but good quality selection of vintage clothing. Owners J.P. and Colleen Ferraioli also run sister store Yesterday's News, at the other end of Court Street.

Other location:
Yesterday's News: 428 Court Street, Carroll Gardens, Brooklyn 11231 (718-875-0546)

$

THE COMMUNITY BOOKSTORE

212 Court Street, Cobble Hill 11201
718-834-9494
Mon-Sun 15:00-23:00 (Aug/Sept closed)
Subway F, G to Bergen Street

For booklovers who miss the days of the secondhand bookshop with racks of 25-cent paperbacks, the Community Bookstore will restore your faith – as long as you are not prone to claustrophobia. Not to be confused with the Community Book Shop in Park Slope, this shop is, frankly, a bit of a dusty mess, with books piled haphazardly and very little space to move about. New books are discounted, but go for the recycled bestsellers, the well-worn classics, and the gems buried in the $1 rack. You won't leave empty-handed.

⑤⑤⑤⑤
DARR

369 Atlantic Avenue, Boerum Hill 11217
718-797-9733
info@shopdarr.com
www.shopdarr.com
Mon-Sat 11:00-19:00; Sun 12:00-18:00
Subway A, C, G to Hoyt-Schermerhorn Streets

This visually stunning shop takes you back to the age of Victorian collectors with its eclectic mix of 'found objects' and its modern Gothic atmosphere. Furniture ranging from Amish to 18th century Moroccan is watched over by unusual vintage taxidermy, Victorian portraits, and anatomical posters, along with botanical specimens displayed under bell jars. Objects range from one-offs to collections of scissors, fans, combs, books, buttons, and pencils, all "carefully arranged as you might in your own home," according to owner Brian Cousins, a former video editor who has teamed up with interior designer Hicham Benmira to scout the world for curiosities. The stock is fluid and can be rented for props – "We re-evaluate as we go," explains Brian – and prices are commensurate with the quality and taste level.

⑤⑤⑤
FORK + PENCIL

221a Court Street, Cobble Hill 11201
718-488-8855
info@forkandpencil.com
www.forkandpencil.com
Tues-Sun 11:00-19:00
Subway F, G to Bergen Street

Fork + Pencil combines quality consignment and donated antiques, old and new housewares, creative children's toys, and gift items that reflect the spirit of Brooklyn's Cobble Hill community; the shop's proceeds are donated to community organizations for the arts, the environment, and the schools. The two-year-old, whitewashed space is charmingly cluttered with vintage plates and glassware, coffee and tea sets, pitchers and candlesticks, spice jars and napkin rings, jewelry and old paintings in a range of prices. Owner Alex Grabcheski recently walked away from his Wall Street job and opened a 3000 square-foot warehouse for his larger antiques around the corner at 18 Bergen Street.

$ $ $ $
RETROFRET/ MUSURGIA

233 Butler Street, Carroll Gardens/ Gowanus 11217
718-237-6092/2532
www.retrofret.com/www.musurgia.com
Mon-Fri 12:00-19:00; Sat 12:00-18:00
Subway F, G to Bergen Street, or R to Union Street

Serious collectors and musicians won't mind making the trek to the historic building in downtown Brooklyn housing luthier Steve Uhrik's New York String Service, a repair service and gallery of museum-quality musical instruments. RetroFret sells vintage, rare and unusual fretted instruments, including electric guitars and amps, steel guitars, 12-string acoustic guitars, banjos, ukuleles, zithers, mandolins, violins and violas. These are lovingly restored on site using vintage tools by RetroFret's head of repair, Mamie Minch. The Musurgia side of the business focuses on musical antiquities, non-Western and experimental musical devices; the name is taken from the 1650 work *Musurgia Universalis*, which catalogued every instrument known at the time. Examples include an 1841 melodian, a 1900 harmonium, 18th century flutes, contra bass sarrusophones, vintage and obsolete brasswinds, an 18th century 'pochette' violin (used for dance classes), and a 1938 theremin. Each of these beautiful instruments has a story to tell.

💲💲💲

STERLING PLACE

363 Atlantic Avenue, Boerum Hill 11217
718-797-5667
customerservice@sterlingplace.com
www.sterlingplace.com
Mon-Fri 11:00-18:30; Sat 11:00-19:00;
Sun 12:00-18:00
Subway A, C, G to Hoyt-Schermerhorn Streets

The focus at Sterling Place is on "artful
objects for gracious giving," with a unique
selection of old and new items, carefully
displayed amongst some beautiful
antiques. There are jewelry, grooming
aids, small leather goods, kitchen and
barware, model toys, picture frames, and
desktop accessories. Many are new, with
a vintage feel, such as a reproduction
Regency floor globe, buffalo nickel
cufflinks, and a selection of Mach 3 razors
with one-of-a-kind antique handles. The
real antiques included an oak Hoosier, a
treadle Singer, and assorted old trunks
and display pieces, such as a set of
tobacco drawers.

💲💲💲

VINTAGE SIGNAGE

334 Atlantic Avenue, Boerum Hill 11201
718-834-9268
Mon-Sun 11:30-19:00
Subway A, C, G to Hoyt-Schermerhorn Streets

Marc and Sylvie, the owners of Vintage
Signage, moved to Brooklyn from France
"so long ago we don't remember," but the
shop retains a certain air of quirky French
chic – just ask the original blue-shirted
Tintin on display. There are vintage
French signs and advertising items from
the restaurant trade, such as ashtrays,
serving trays, tins, corkscrews, menu
boards, wooden bottle cases, glassware
and china, even French café furniture; and
a 1900 *boîte aux lettres*. Marc and Sylvie
also have a passion for music, and there
is an impressive collection of LPs, music
posters and memorabilia on display. Retro
radios, lamps, clocks, photos and a host of
unexpected treasures make this a cheerful
and charming place to shop, and prices
are reasonable.

$ $

UGLY LUGGAGE

214 Bedford Avenue, Williamsburg 11211
718-384-0724
uglyluggage@gmail.com
Mon-Fri 13:00-20:00; Sat/Sun 12:00-19:00
Subway L to Bedford Avenue

Ugly Luggage has been Williamsburg's
go-to shop for cool furniture and
collectibles since 1993 – before the
neighborhood became the home of the
hip. It's an eclectic jumble from granny's
attic: furniture, old toys, cameras
and mechanical typewriters, pretty
lampshades and glassware, mirrors,
steamer trunks and, yes, ugly luggage.
Photographers and stylists source
nostalgic props here, such as a giant
wooden dough bowl; and I found a Ranger
Joe mug and cereal bowl just like the one
I had in the 50s.

HOME & INTERIORS

*Home Furnishings / Décor
Lighting / Bicycles / Salvage*

FROM BROOKLYN'S BROWNSTONES TO TRIBECA'S CAST-IRON LOFTS, FROM PRE-WAR PARK AVENUE BRICK TO THE MODERN GLASS TOWERS SPRINGING UP ALL OVER THE CITY, NEW YORK'S TRANSIENT APARTMENT DWELLERS ARE CONSTANTLY REDECORATING. LACK OF STORAGE SPACE CREATES A CONSTANT FLOW OF SECONDHAND AND VINTAGE FURNITURE AND HOME DÉCOR CIRCULATING THROUGH THE SHOPS, FROM HIGH-END ANTIQUE GALLERIES TO CHARITY AND THRIFT SHOPS AND EVEN THE FLEA MARKETS; AND THERE ARE OCCASIONALLY TREASURES TO BE FOUND ON THE SIDEWALKS WORTH TAKING HOME AND REFURBISHING.

Architectural salvage is another rich source of secondhand and vintage décor, including beautiful mantelpieces, mirrors, windows, metalwork, plumbing and lighting fixtures from some of New York's landmark buildings that have sadly been razed or gutted for new endeavors. Whether you are looking for serious antiques, mid-century modern, or shabby chic, there's plenty to choose from for the house and garden.

💲💲💲💲

NEW YORK GALLERIES ANTIQUES

111 West 25th Street, Chelsea 10001
212-352-1819
Mon-Sun 10:00-18:00
Subway 1, F, M, N, R to 23rd Street,
or 1, N, R to 28th Street

This well-established (since 1976) shop stocks some serious antiques including a magnificent selection of chandeliers and ornamental lighting, along with whimsical marble and majolica pieces, and interesting art, crystal, china and silver. Owner Lonnie Coffman is an outspoken supporter of the Chelsea neighborhood's secondhand scene. Hours may vary, so please call ahead.

💲💲💲 - 💲💲💲💲

OLDE GOOD THINGS

124 West 24th Street, Chelsea 10011
212-989-8401
mail@oldegoodthings.com
www.ogtstore.com
Mon-Sun 10:00-19:00
Subway 1, F, M, N, R to 23rd Street

With three locations in Manhattan and two in Los Angeles, a presence at Brooklyn Flea and other East Coast flea markets, and a warehouse in Scranton, Pennsylvania, this is the place to go for architectural salvage and altered antiques. "The most interesting stores in New York" feature old chandeliers, sconces, and pressed tin ceiling tiles from renovated brownstones; a large selection of mantels including a hand-picked marble collection from the recent Plaza Hotel renovation; and beautiful windows from New York monuments such as the Park Avenue Armory and the Flatiron Building. At the 9000 square-foot Chelsea store, cases full of doorknobs and roses, drawer pulls, hinges and lockplates line the walls. Ornate banisters, gilt-framed mirrors, celestial statuary and enormous clocks from hotel lobbies create a neo-Gothic ambiance. The organization is owned and managed by the Church of Bible Understanding, an evangelical Christian group.

Other locations:
5 East 16th Street 10003
(212-989-8814)

450 Columbus Avenue 10024
(212-362-8025)

$ $ $ $

SECONDHAND ROSE

230 Fifth Avenue, suite 510,
Midtown West 10001
212-393-9002
shroseltd@aol.com
www.secondhandrose.com
Mon-Fri 10:00-18:00
Subway N, R, 6 to 28th Street

$ $ $

PIPPIN VINTAGE HOME

112½ West 17th Street, Chelsea 10011
212-505-5159
info@pippinvintage.com
www.pippinvintage.com
Mon-Sat 11:00-19:00; Sun 12:00-18:00
Subway F, M to 14th Street,
L to Sixth Avenue, or 1 to 18th Street

Next door to Pippin Vintage Jewelry
(see p17) you will find the charming
courtyard and miniature country house
that is Pippin Vintage Home. Cozy sofas,
antique mirrors, old bureaus and storage
trunks create a homey atmosphere as you
browse amongst drawers of old buttons
and shelves of pretty glassware. We loved
the Art Nouveau repoussé buckles as well
as a tea set from the 1890s. Owners Rachel
and Steve Cooper live in bucolic western
Massachusetts, where they source their
unique stock at reasonable prices.

Vintage wallpaper specialist Secondhand
Rose has been in business for almost 50
years, originally in the West Village, then
in Tribeca, and now in a fifth-floor shop in
Manhattan's décor and gift district. Owner
Suzanne Lipschutz offers over 5000
patterns, most from the 1940s, 50s and
60s; with some small runs from as early
as the 1870s. The papers are organized in
books, by style: florals, geometrics, flocks,
damasks, Mylars, Chinoiserie, scenics,
faux finishes, etc., and manager Martin
Dinowitz knows the bin location for each
and every one. The shop originally sold
linoleum and furniture as well, and some
choice pieces, primarily of Persian origin,
are on display in current quarters.

$$$

LANDMARK VINTAGE BICYCLES

136 East Third Street, East Village 10009
212-674-2343
mail@landmarkbicycles.com
www.landmarkbicycles.com
Mon-Fri 11:00-20:00; Sat/Sun 11:00-18:00
Subway 6 to Astor Place,
or F, M to Second Avenue

Opened in 2008, Landmark supplies
New York's booming population of bike
enthusiasts with "vintage bikes that you
can ride every day." The shop carries lug
frame, all-steel vintage bikes from the
late 1950s to the 1980s, many of them
exclusive and/or customized; and there
are usually about 100 bikes on the floor
from which to choose, including models
from Raleigh, Schwinn, Peugeot, and
Sears, and Japanese bikes. Parts,
repairs and refurbishments are a
big part of the business.

$$$$$
LOST CITY ARTS

18 Cooper Square, East Village 10003
212-375-0500
lostcityarts@yahoo.com
www.lostcityarts.com
Mon-Fri 10:00-18:00; Sat/Sun 12:00-18:00
Subway N, R to Eighth Street,
or 6 to Astor Place

Owner James Elkind describes his homage to mid-century modern as "a melding of the post-war decorative and fine arts," and travels the world in search of art furniture, lighting, modern art and sculpture. Located across the square from the renowned Cooper Union (a college of art, architecture and engineering), Lost City Arts is appreciated by the area's design-focused clientele. It features tactile and sculptural furniture by the likes of Eames, Nakashima, and Scandinavian designers; along with eccentric and modernist art, including a fine collection of Harry Bertoia prints and sculpture. European lighting is another specialty, from Art Deco and Murano lamps to Danish Modern pendants and sputnik-inspired chandeliers from the 1970s. More a gallery than a shop, prices are commensurate with the quality and often one-of-a-kind stock. "It's necessary to sell, but the fun part is searching and collecting," says Elkind. "Sourcing material is endlessly fascinating."

$
RECYCLE-A-BICYCLE

75 Avenue C, East Village 10009
212-475-1655
www.recycleabicycle.org
Mon-Sat 12:00-19:00; Sun 12:00-17:00
Subway F, M to Second Avenue,
or 6 to Astor Pl

This non-profit organization ticks all the boxes: it refurbishes donations of used bicycles, diverting some 1200 bicycles annually from landfill; it offers employment, job training, and environmental education to youth in partnership with the schools and other community organizations; its Earn-A-Bike program allows student volunteers to earn bikes for themselves and their families; and its Kids Ride Club takes city kids on group rides, providing cycles and helmets and teaching bike safety and healthy lifestyles. Proceeds from its two shops go directly into these programs while providing the bike-riding public with affordable, reconditioned bicycles. Why wouldn't you buy a bike here?

⑤⑤⑤

THE UPPER RUST

445 East Ninth Street, East Village 10009
212-533-3953
Wed-Mon 12:00-19:00
Subway L to First Avenue, or 6 to Astor Place

Treasures from estate sales spill onto the sidewalks of Kevin Bockrath's house and garden emporium. A jumble of old and new, the look is a mix of Southern Living and shabby chic charm. Country dressers, curio cabinets, and dressing tables display collections of jewelry, picture frames, mercury glass, soup tureens, cookie jars, old biscuit tins and spools of yarn. Painted mirrors and light fixtures, wicker and rocking chairs, candelabra and vintage clocks, posters and postcards fill every available space. There are affordable accessories here as well as higher-priced furniture and collectibles.

⑤⑤⑤⑤

OCHRE

462 Broome Street, SoHo 10013
212-414-4332
info@ochrestore.com
www.ochrestore.com
Mon-Sat 11:00-19:00; Sun 12:00-18:00
Subway N, R to Prince Street,
or 6 to Spring Street

The offspring of a London-based furniture and lighting design company, Ochre Store features a contemporary range as well as vintage items for the home. Sourced globally, the well-made and refined decorative objects have a hand-crafted aesthetic, often based in natural materials. There's something for everyone here at a wide range of price points, from a set of vintage Indian lassi cups, to a pair of kidney-shaped mid-century Danish candleholders, and a 12-foot-high, 19th century pine vitrine from France. Refurbished silver, vintage linens, and recycled glassware mix with contemporary wood and ceramic pieces and Ochre's own line of furniture and lighting, making this shop a very pleasant place indeed.

$ $ $ $ $

LAS VENUS

163 Ludlow Street, Lower East Side 10002
212-982-0608
www.lasvenus.com
Mon-Fri 11:00-19:00; Sat/Sun 12:00-19:00
Subway F, J, M, Z to Delancey & Essex Streets

This celebration of 1960s and 70s décor opened in 1995 at the cusp of the Lower East Side renaissance, and now has two additional branches full of colorful, outrageous pieces of furniture, modern art and pop culture, all in top-notch condition. It's a popular place for fashion shoots, music videos, and set designers – think Austin Powers. Shag rugs, sputnik lamps, Danish modern and chrome tables, graphic mirrors and art glass collectibles are punctuated with showcase items such as a Pierre Cardin metal sequin screen or a Venini crystal chandelier, and signature pieces by mid-century modern designers such as Paul Evans and Michael Coffey. While these are serious investment pieces, you can also find more affordable *objets d'art* here.

Other locations:
LV2 at 113 Stanton Street, 10002
(212-358-8000)

Las Venus at ABC 888 Broadway, 10003
(212-473-3000 ext.519)

$ $ $ $

CIRCA ANTIQUES, LTD

374 Atlantic Avenue, Boerum Hill 11217
718-596-1866
circa@circaantiquesltd.com
www.circaantiquesltd.com
Tues-Sat 11:00-18:00; Sun 12:00-18:00
Subway A, C, G to Hoyt-Schermerhorn Streets

For 36 years Rachel Leibowicz and David
Goldstein have specialized in quality 19th
century American and Victorian furniture
and accessories sourced from estate
sales as well as from some of Brooklyn's
fine old brownstones. Pieces such as an
1840s pigeon-holed rolltop desk signed
by J. & J.W. Meeks, or an American Oak
moondial grandfather clock from 1902, are
of serious caliber; and the shop also offers
restoration and repair work if necessary.
The unintimidating owners are happy to
share their knowledge, and the shop not
only contains spectacular chandeliers,
Tiffany glass, and assorted art; it is also
full of lovely porcelain, glassware, and
silver pieces priced for collecting or
gifting, such as a strawberry pink and
gold Royal Worcester cheesekeeper
from 1865. We would have been happy to
own the pretty silver vanity set or any of
the Wedgwood or pewter knick-knacks.
"People do come here from far, far away,"
acknowledged Rachel; we can see why.

$ $ $ $

CITY FOUNDRY

365 Atlantic Avenue, Boerum Hill 11217
718-923-1786/718-812-3335
cityfoundry@aol.com
www.cityfoundry.com
Tues-Thu by appointment;
Fri-Sun 11:00-19:00
Subway A, C, G to Hoyt-Schermerhorn Streets

Opened in 2000, City Foundry (or CF), was one of the first antiques shops along Brooklyn's Atlantic Avenue, and quickly gained a following among urban loft dwellers with its emphasis on mid-century modern and industrial artifacts. Owner Sohrab Bakhshi describes himself as "obsessed" with his unique collection of modern furniture, industrial lighting, tools and toys, storage units and safes, media props, and more; he works closely with set designers from TV, film, retail venues and restaurants. Bakhshi originally studied furniture-making, then turned to collecting unique furniture and objects – "Everyone wanted to buy, so I decided to set up a shop." Far from feeling chaotic, the selection of weights and scales, robots and drafting tools, kitchen clocks and anatomical posters are carefully curated and displayed, along with important Danish modern tables and wrought-iron garden furniture. While its prices can seem high, the shop gets good press for its design cred and appreciation of industrial design.

HORSEMAN ANTIQUES

351 Atlantic Avenue, Boerum Hill 11217
718-596-1048
horseman.antiques@gmail.com
www.horsemanantiques.net
Mon-Fri 10:00-19:00; Sat 11:00-19:00;
Sun 12:00-19:00
Subway A, C, G to Hoyt-Schermerhorn Streets

With five floors and 25,000 square feet of Victorian to mid-century modern and industrial furniture, it is easy to get lost in Horseman Antiques. Established in 1962, the shop boasts an extensive collection of leaded stained glass windows and doors, along with bronze statuary, industrial metal furniture and lighting, Danish modern, and random antiques stacked to the rafters. While there are no prices in sight, each piece sports a catalogue number; and the old adage "if you have to ask, you can't afford it," applies here. Nevertheless, the international selection is worth perusing if you enjoy the process of furnishing your home with unusual finds. Horseman Antiques also has a New Jersey warehouse for their "globally acquired inventory"; they will ship internationally, and rent pieces for New York's film, theatre and television productions.

TIME GALLERIES

562 Fifth Avenue, Park Slope 11215
718-788-8300
timegalleries@aol.com
Mon-Sat 09:00-18:00; Sun 12:00-18:00
Subway R to Prospect Avenue

This shop is a furniture lover's dream: two floors stacked high with antique furniture, lighting, rugs and paintings, and an on-site repair shop. Sourced mostly from estate sales, there's everything from a zinc-topped pine kitchen table to a Victorian rolltop secretary, 19th century French chandeliers, or an Ethan Allen toile-covered sofa. The atmosphere isn't fancy, but the selection of dressers, sideboards, armoires and tables at fair prices will satisfy the dedicated shopper.

$\$\$$ – $\$\$\$$

SANFORD AND SVEN'S SECOND HAND

106 North Third Street, Williamsburg 11249
718-487-9806
sven@sanfordandsven.com
www.sanfordandsven.com
Tues-Sun 13:00-19:30
Subway L to Bedford Avenue

If you are old enough to remember a certain TV series from the 70s about a junkman and his son, then Sanford and Sven's garage will make you smile with nostalgia. The furniture ranges from shabby to chic – rocking chairs, bureaus, dining tables and sideboards – but there are some real bargains on the big pieces; and there are shelves full of old typewriters, cameras, TVs, sewing machines, movie projectors, etc. You'll also find a really nice collection of cookie jars; antique cobbler's tools; and some lovely pressed or cut glass *objets*. Hours may vary so call ahead if it's on your must list.

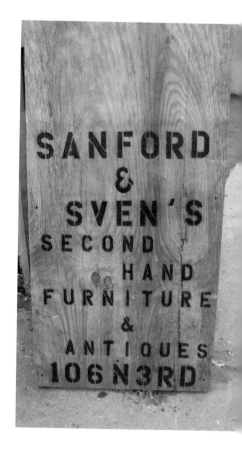

ONLY IN
NEW YORK

*Thrift Shops / Flea Markets
Unique Traders*

NEW YORK'S WHIMSICAL THRIFT SHOPS AND FLEA MARKETS ARE NOT ONLY A GREAT SOURCE FOR BARGAINS; THEY ALSO PROVIDE HOURS OF SHOPPING ENTERTAINMENT. MOST (BUT NOT ALL) THRIFT SHOPS RAISE MONEY FOR CHARITABLE ORGANIZATIONS SUCH AS SCHOOLS, CHURCHES, OR VARIOUS HIGH-PROFILE DISEASES. SOCIETY MATRONS HAVE TRADITIONALLY SUPPORTED THESE CAUSES BY DONATING THEIR GENTLY-WORN FINERY AND GOOD-QUALITY HOME FURNISHINGS; AND SHOPPERS CAN SCORE HIGH-END MERCHANDISE FOR A FRACTION OF NEW VALUE AT THE MORE SELECT SHOPS. OTHER THRIFTS ACCEPT DONATIONS OF PRACTICALLY ANYTHING, AND WHILE THERE ARE SOME AMAZING BARGAINS, THE WISE SHOPPER WILL CAST A CRITICAL EYE BEFORE BUYING.

New York's weekend flea markets have exploded in the past few years as high shop rents have made things difficult for established small retailers and new entrepreneurs alike. Secondhand clothing, furniture and collectibles mix with arts and crafts and gourmet food stalls in a family atmosphere, providing a great day out. New flea markets keep popping up; it's worthwhile checking the Internet for new spots such as the Hester Street Market and the DeKalb Market.

For creative types, New York's garment center offers a unique range of stores full of fabrics and trims, both old and new. Many are sample yardages specially developed or sourced for the city's clothing and costume designers over the years. There are additional shops and markets linked with the city's history, such as the 47th Street Diamond District, that can be found only in New York, and are worth a visit.

$ $

ARTHRITIS FOUNDATION THRIFT SHOP

1430 Third Avenue, Upper East Side 10028
212-722-8816
www.arthritis.org
Mon-Sat 10:00-18:00; Sun 12:00-17:00
Subway 4, 5, 6 to 86th Street

This shop's recent castoffs from the ladies-who-lunch comprise shoes from Manolo, Moschino, Miu Miu and Prada; bags from Le Sport Sac and Nine West; designer scarves; and a host of pretty chapeaus. Dresses from Upper East Side favorites such as Lily Pulitzer, Nicole Miller, Rena Lange and Diane Von Furstenburg include some never worn merchandise. A local institution, whose proceeds benefit the Arthritis Foundation, the shop also features silver, jewelry, and small bric-a-brac.

💲💲
CANCER*CARE* THRIFT SHOP

1480 Third Avenue, Upper East Side 10028
212-879-9868
www.cancercare.org
Mon/Tues/Fri 11:00-18:00; Wed/
Thu 11:00-19:00; Sat 11:00-16:30;
Sun 12:30-17.00
Subway 4, 5, 6 to 86th Street

Like its thrift-shop neighbors along
Third Avenue, donations at Cancer*Care*
reflect the neighborhood's generally
prosperous denizens, but the hunt for
treasure requires some patience. On the
day of our visit we found a fabulous array
of fur, sheepskin, and wool coats from the
likes of Armani and Cinzia Rocca; along
with tweedy suits, designer scarves and
after-five wear. China and bric-a-brac here
were better than elsewhere. Cancer*Care* is
a national organization offering support
and resources to those affected by cancer.

💲💲
COUNCIL THRIFT SHOP

246 East 84th Street, Upper East Side 10028
212-439-8373
www.ncjwny.org
Mon-Wed 11:00-17:45; Thu 11:00-19:45;
Fri/Sat 11:00-16:45
Subway 4, 5, 6 to 86th Street

Run by the New York Council of Jewish
Women and benefitting a range of
community charities, the Council Thrift
Shop is jammed with furniture and
household goods as well as clothing
at thrifty prices. Luggage and linens,
golf clubs and glassware, fur coats and
wheelchairs, designer kit and kitchenware,
toys and games, books, records and CDs
make this a fun place to shop.

⑤⑤⑤
GREENFLEA

Columbus Avenue and West 77th Street,
Upper West Side 10024
212-239-3025
greenflea@aol.com
www.greenfleamarkets.com
Sun 10:00-17:45
Subway 1 to 79th Street

GreenFlea was incorporated in 1985 by the parents' associations of two local schools to raise funds for the enrichment of their children's education. With both indoor and outdoor facilities, the market is an uptown mix of antiques, artistry and repurposed treasures that attracts a grown-up crowd of cognoscenti. At Visually Vintage you'll find racks of Whiting & Davis bags as well as vintage cufflinks and marcasite jewelry. Garden's Edge Antiques features antique glassware and silver pieces; we found a John Maddock covered tureen and Fostoria wine goblets. Wild Rose Antiques (nycwildrose@yahoo.com) specializes in shabby chic found and refinished furniture. Pat Haber's Fabulous Furs were selling even on a hot July day; her beaded 1920s flapper dresses and white cotton Victorian chemises looked more seasonal. At SoléArts (www.solearts.com) Diane DiRaimo fashions delicate jewelry from red, yellow and green traffic light lenses and recycled watch gears. Scott Jordan salvages bits of old pottery and glass for his New York Artifact Art jewelry (www.newyorkartifactart.com). The Treasure Hunter collects antique bottles, marbles, buttons, and Matchbox cars from the 60s and 70s. Jian Wei Chen's beautiful bone chess sets, delicate dominoes and Mah-Jongg tiles, carved and lacquered boxes, coral necklaces and calligraphy brushes were most unusual. Indoors GreenFlea offers lots of jewelry, silver, tableware and glass, along with vintage greeting cards, decals and Currier & Ives prints. Maurice Christian's collection of antique timepieces includes pocket watches from the 19th century as well as mid-century models from Longines, Tissot, Hamilton and Omega.

"I JUST LOVE OLD LACE AND ROSES – THEY CAN COVER ANY MISTAKE"

Jennifer Toledo, *Wild Rose Antiques*

Wild Rose Antiques at GreenFlea

Imagine a dream of a white-on-white bedroom, furnished with a hand-carved bedframe, oversized bureaus and armoires, gilded mirrors, hand-tatted dresser scarves, and cut-glass perfume bottles. Born and raised in New York's West Side, Wild Rose Antiques' owner Jennifer Toledo has been collecting the pieces of this dream all her life. "It's the treasure hunting that I love," she explains.

Now living on a 50-acre farm in southern New Jersey, Jennifer and her partner Bill are regulars at the region's auction houses. Everything at Wild Rose Antiques is vintage; everything is refinished in a signature shade of white. "I just love old lace and roses – they can cover any mistake," she declares. The furniture is reasonably priced, and there are plenty of pretties such as satin lingerie and fluttery fans that will fit in a shopping bag.

NEW YORK ARTIFACT ART AT GREENFLEA

Scott Jordan is a digger and a self-taught historian and archaeologist who's spent much of his life searching through New York's never-ending urban renewal for a bit of the past. Over the years he's accumulated a collection of old bottles, pottery, keys, toys, shoes and other items, some dating as far back as the 17th century, which form a patchwork history of the city. Scott's passion for preserving New York's history is detailed in his book, *Past Objects*.

At GreenFlea, Scott offers a collection of jewelry, designed and handmade by Dolhathai S (also known as Pooh) from old buttons, bits of glass and shards of pottery. Each item comes with an explanation of its provenance; for example, the privy well of 40 Perry Street, or the landfill at Greenpoint, Brooklyn. Scott also specializes in restoration of larger pieces. "Our aim is to save the past and share with the public," he says.

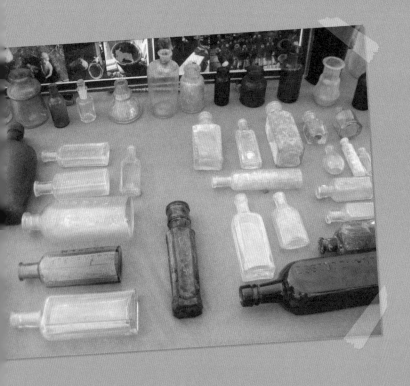

$$

MEMORIAL SLOAN-KETTERING THRIFT SHOP

1440 Third Avenue, Upper East Side 10028
212-535-1250
http://mskcc.convio.net
Mon-Wed 10:00-17:30; Thu 10:00-18:00;
Sat 11:00-17:00; Sun 12:00-17:00
Subway 4, 5, 6 to 86th Street

With proceeds benefitting patient care, research and education programs at Memorial Sloan-Kettering's cancer center, this well-established and tidy thrift shop reflects its Upper East Side setting with a seasonal array of women's and men's clothing, shoes, bags and costume jewelry, as well as books, small furnishings and household art. Much of the stock is gently-worn 'occasion' clothing, a few years out of date. However, there are occasional vintage treasures such as a 1930s satin wedding gown. To be fair, the shop was in seasonal changeover the day of our visit, and in this neighborhood most thrift shops turn over a good number of designer pieces.

$$

SPENCE-CHAPIN THRIFT SHOP

1473 Third Avenue, Upper East Side 10028
212-737-8448
www.spence-chapin.org
Mon-Fri 11:00-18:00; Sat 11:00-17:00;
Sun 12:00-17:00
Subway 4, 5, 6 to 86th Street

Benefitting the Spence-Chapin organization's services for orphanages and adoption programs, the shop sells high-end secondhand clothing donated by label-conscious neighborhood residents, as well as new merchandise donated by various New York designers and retailers; a collection of sample garments from Diane Von Furstenberg Studio was featured on the day of our visit. It was nice to see a section devoted to plus size clothing here as well. There was also a great collection of men's Ferragamo ties and dress shirts from the likes of Pink and Zegna.

$ $ $

B&J FABRICS

**525 Seventh Avenue, 2nd floor, Midtown
West 10018
212-354-8150
info@bandjfabrics.com
www.bandjfabrics.com
Mon-Fri 08:00-17:45; Sat 09:00-16:45
Subway 1, 2, 3, 7, N, R, Q, S to
Times Square-42nd Street**

Offering designer-quality fabrics by the yard, this garment center institution is a must for amateur seamstresses, tailors, design students and costume designers. Started by the Cohen brothers in 1940, the business originally dealt in remnants left over from the war effort. Now sourcing fabrics from hundreds of vendors from around the world, there is a focus on continuity, as well as spectacular one-offs from the archives and overruns from New York's designers. "We never buy for price – it's here because we want it here," insists third-generation family member Scot Cohen. Linens and laces, tweeds and tulles, sequins and silks, prints and plaids, brocades, velvets and much more will find you spoilt for choice.

$ $ $

THE GARAGE ANTIQUE FLEA MARKET

112 West 25th Street, Chelsea 10001
212-243-5343
info@hellskitchenfleamarket.com
www.hellskitchenfleamarket.com
Sat/Sun 09:00-17:00
Subway 1, F, M, N, R to 23rd Street,
or 1, N, R to 28th Street

Also known as The Antiques Garage, this old parking garage is chock-a-block with around 100 vendors of trash and treasures spread over two floors. Prices range accordingly from $15 to $2000, but there are some quality finds here. At Pickers Barn, Matthew showed us his collection of *objets d'vertu* including antique metal Bavarian buttons, vintage eyeglasses, gold or silver-topped walking sticks, and a late 19th century glass eye. Elsewhere we found nautical collectibles, ship's lanterns and sextants from the 40s and 50s at The

Hesperus Nauticals (www.thehesperus.com); African masks and carvings from Cameroon at Kanda African Art (www.kandaarts.com); old prayer books and rosaries, telescopes and binoculars; and designer clothing for men and women, as well as crinolines and lacy bits. Upstairs booths featured jewelry and watches, rare books and comics, old cameras and photos, theatrical costumes and rolls of flocked wallpapers, bird and botanical prints. The Garage was started in 1994 by Alan Boss, owner of Hell's Kitchen Flea Market and the West 25th Street Market nearby. While the building has unfortunately been sold, the Garage is now operating on a month-to-month lease. If and when the Garage closes its doors, its vendors will be offered space in the other two sites.

HELL'S KITCHEN FLEA MARKET

West 39th Street between Ninth and Tenth Avenues, Midtown West 10018
212-243-5343
www.hellskitchenfleamarket.com
Sat-Sun 09:00-18:00 (weather permitting)
Subway A, C, E to Port Authority-42nd Street

Set behind New York's Port Authority Bus Terminal amidst the highways and viaducts, you'd be forgiven for thinking the Hell's Kitchen Flea Market was the setting for an urban disaster movie. Described in the 19th century as "the lowest and filthiest neighborhood in the city," these days the area known as Clinton is home to actors, theatres, food markets and restaurants. This is definitely an old school flea market, with around 50 vendors of the cheap and cheerful, unique and unusual. The Bad Boys of 39th Street specialize in 'mantiques' such as old tools, antique typewriters, and primitive snowshoes. There are booths with old LPs, posters, picture frames, naïve art, steamer

trunks, doorknobs and roses, locks and keys; we stumbled across pieces of 1940s McCoy pottery in signature yellows, blues and greens. Wildpalm Vintage Jewelry (www.wildpalmvintage.com) feature pearl-embroidered lace collars from the 50s, perfect for topping your cardi, as well as boldly beaded collars and cuffs from India. It would be hard to beat the selection of classic Coach and Dooney & Bourke bags at Citi Chic. "Now that Coach is reissuing, everyone is coming for these," confides owner Grace Wilson. City Chic also offers Doc Martens and L.L. Bean boots, along with choice vintage garments. There are no price tags; "Pricing is negotiable," according to Grace.

$ HOUSING WORKS

143 West 17th Street, Chelsea 10011
718-838-5050
info@housingworks.org
www.housingworks.org
Mon-Fri 10:00-19:00; Sat 10:00-18:00;
Sun 12:00-17:00
Subway F, M, to 14th Street, L to Sixth
Avenue, or 1 to 18th Street

The Housing Works thrift shops –
there are 12 of them scattered across
Manhattan and Brooklyn – are part of
an organization that provides housing
and support for New York's victims of
AIDS and HIV. The shops are staffed by
cheerful volunteers and are jammed with
contemporary secondhand clothing and
household goods at bargain prices. At
the Chelsea store, clothing, shoes and
jewelry were merchandised by color, with
brands ranging from designer to mass
market. Furniture ranged from medicine
cabinets to armoires and antique pine
dressers. Price tags were explained in
terms of the value of a service supplied
by the organization. For example, a dress
was marked "This is the price of a hot
meal," and the tag for a cherry hutch top
declared "This is essential health care."
Housing Works Thrift Shops are found
in Gramercy, SoHo, the West Village,
Tribeca, Hell's Kitchen, the Upper East
and West Side, Brooklyn Heights and
Park Slope. Please check the website for
individual locations and opening hours.

$ $ $
HYMAN HENDLER & SONS

21 West 38th Street, Midtown West 10018
212-840-8393
ribbons58@aol.com
www.hymanhendler.com
Mon-Fri 09:00-17:00
Subway B, D, F, M, 7 to 42nd Street-Bryant
Park, or B, D, F, M, Q, R, N to
34th Street-Herald Square

This treasure trove of beautiful vintage ribbons is located in Manhattan's Garment Center, but was born over 100 years ago as a pushcart business on the city's Lower East Side. There's an array of bespoke and archival ribbons of all description: grosgrain, moiré, velvet, satin, taffeta, picot edge, plaids, jacquard novelties, and much more, many from now-defunct European mills. Now managed by third-generation family member Michael Weisman, the company houses additional stock in a 15,000 square-foot warehouse in Queens. This shop is a one-of-a-kind resource for fashion, bridal and event designers, as well as for the millinery and decorative trades.

$ $ $ $ $
NEW YORK DIAMOND DISTRICT

West 47th Street between Fifth and
Sixth Avenues, Midtown West 10036
www.nydiamonddistrict.com
Check individual stores for hours;
many open every day
Subway B, D, F, M to 47th-50th Streets
Rockefeller Center

Founded in the 1920s by jewelers from the Bowery, Canal and Fulton Streets, New York's Diamond District is one of the world's largest centers for diamonds and fine jewelry, containing hundreds of diamond dealers, jewelry manufacturers, wholesalers, retailers, estate jewelers and pawn shops within the city block. Many are 'family jewelers' who have long-term relationships with their clients; and it helps to have an introduction if you are looking for the best. Not for the faint-hearted, this is where one shops for serious bling.

💲💲💲

ROSEN & CHADICK FABRICS

561 Seventh Avenue, 2nd & 3rd floor, Midtown West 10018
212-869-0142
www.rosenandchadickfabrics.com
Mon-Fri 08:30-17:45; Sat 09:00-16:30
Subway 1, 2, 3, 7, N, R, Q, S to Times Square-42nd Street

Since 1952 this family-owned fabric store has served the students and designers of New York's garment center and theatre district, and a visit here is a must for sewing enthusiasts. There are woolens, printed silks, and velvets both vintage and modern; Chanel-type tweeds; glittering foils and lames; as well as a large selection of charming printed cottons that are ideal for quilters and crafters. Choose from the archives, including overruns from New York's design studios, and upcycle these one-of-a-kind fabric finds into your own fabulous design. While the two floors of gorgeous fabric can result in sensory overload, Ellen Rosen and David Chadick are happy to help you put your project together.

$$$$$

SHOWPLACE DESIGN + ANTIQUE CENTER

40 West 25th Street, Chelsea 10001
212-633-6063
info@nyshowplace.com
www.nyshowplace.com
Mon-Fri 10:00-18:00; Sat/Sun 08:30-15:30
Subway 1, F, M, N, R to 23rd Street

When the weather makes perusing the flea markets unpleasant, head for this upscale indoor assemblage of antiques and vintage finds with some 200 galleries spread over four floors. You'll find serious bling and fabulous brooches at Ira Scheck (irascheck@aol.com) (Gallery 25/26) and Roberta's Antique Jewelry (rena.bach@gmail.com) (Gallery 11); vintage watches and timepieces at Tempvs Fvgit (www.tempvsfvgit.com) (Gallery 29); and 10,000 pairs of cufflinks at The Missing Link (www.missinglinknyc.com) (Gallery 108). Marlene Wetherell (marlenewetherell@aol.com) (Gallery 210) specializes in vintage couture from the likes of St Laurent, Dior, Lagerfeld, Chloe, and Alaïa; we loved a sequined Bill Blass cricket sweater. Lisa Farago's collection of original vintage posters from turn-of-the-century and Art Deco Europe includes artists such as Toulouse-Lautrec, Mucha, Cappiello, Gruau, Razzia and Villemot at Farago Art (www.faragoart.com) (Gallery 208). A veritable history of communications takes center stage at Waves LLC (www.wavesllc.com) (Gallery 107), starring old radios and microphones, phonographs, telephones, televisions and a turn-of-the-century Blickensderfer 5 typewriter. If you dream of *Mad Men* and 1950s homemakers, Mood Indigo (www.moodindigonewyork.com) (Gallery 222) overflows with cocktail paraphernalia, ashtrays and barware, salt and pepper shakers, anodized aluminum pieces, Fiestaware, Russel Wright dinnerware and Bakelite. There's a wide range of booths featuring period art and collectibles from around the globe, including Russian art and religious icons from the 17th to the 19th century at ARTvkg (artvkg@yahoo.com) (Gallery 128). The center's top floor is an eclectic collection of Victorian to mid-century modern furniture, lighting and art. While the center is open every day, many of the galleries set their own hours, including by special appointment; so check with individual dealers.

§§§
TINSEL TRADING COMPANY

1 West 37th Street, Midtown West 10018
212-730-1030
tinseltrading@juno.com
www.tinseltrading.com
Mon-Fri 09:45-18:00; Sat 11:00-17:00
Subway B, D, F, M, 7 to 42nd Street-Bryant
Park, or B, D, F, M, Q, R, N to 34th Street-
Herald Square

All that glitters is at Tinsel Trading
Company, along with a vast collection
of trims, tassels, badges, buttons and
ornaments from the past. In 1933
young Arch Bergoffen purchased the
French Tinsel Company in Manhattan,
an importer of metal threads in all
sizes and colors that were used for
military uniforms. In 1969 the business
transitioned from wholesale to retail
with a storefront in New York's Garment
Center, beloved by fashion and home
designers and the nearby theatre
community for its spectacular array of
metallic ribbons and trims. Bergoffen's
granddaughter, Marcia Ceppos, has
organized, updated, and moved the
collection to its current home, where
you'll find metallic ribbons, vintage
passementerie, antique appliqués in
sequins, raffia or chenille, and treasures
in tinsel beyond your wildest dreams.

§§
WEST 25TH STREET MARKET

29-37 West 25th Street, Chelsea 10001
212-243-5343
info@hellskitchenfleamarket.com
www.hellskitchenfleamarket.com
Sat-Sun 09:00-17:00
Subway 1, F, M, N, R to 23rd Street,
or N, R to 28th Street

While the parking-lot site is pretty gritty,
there are bargains to be had, from coral
handle calligraphy brushes and carved
fetishes to watches and jewelry, eyewear,
old bicycles and record albums, as well
as furniture, vintage clothing (including
some lovely 1930s beaded chiffon pieces),
paper ephemera, and African and Tibetan
tribal artifacts. Prices are negotiable. This
sibling of the Antiques Garage should
gain additional vendors and improved
status if and when the Garage is forced
to close.

Ⓢ

CAUZ FOR PAWZ

212 East 23rd Street, Gramercy Park 10010
212-684-7299
www.cauzforpawz.com
Mon-Sat 10:00-19:30; Sun 11:00-18:00
Subway 6, N, R to 23rd Street

This recent addition to Thrift Row uses
its proceeds to promote the well-being of
animals through funding and supplying
animal shelters and veterinarian services.
While the donations range from basic
men's dress shirts and slacks and women's
clothing from the likes of GAP, Loft and
J.Crew, to attractive costume jewelry,
men's ties, outerwear and shoes, the prices
are hard to beat. With a few exceptions,
merchandise is organized and priced
by category (jeans, sweaters, tops, etc.),
and a bargain basement is loaded with
incredibly cheap housewares and linens,
toys and games, small appliances and
cookware, clothing and books.

Ⓢ

GOODWILL STORE

220 East 23rd Street, Gramercy Park 10010
212-447-7270
www.goodwillny.org
Mon-Sat 10:00-20:00; Sun 10:00-19:00

Goodwill Industries is a century-old,
non-sectarian organization dedicated to
helping people achieve participation in
society through employment. Its thrift
shops are well-known for accepting all
manner of donations from on-the-move
New Yorkers, with several sites in the
city. The cheerful and well-lit 23rd Street
thrift shop is notable for its location along
Gramercy's Thrift Row. Clean, cheap
clothing is plentiful here, organized and
priced by rack, including ladies sweaters,
coats, and jeans, along with shoes, belts
and bags. There's a large selection of
children's clothes and necessities such as
high chairs, strollers and toys, as well as
overstocks in bedding, slippers, and socks
and underwear piled in bins. The selection
of small appliances and furnishings
includes TVs, vacuum cleaners, folding
chairs, ironing boards, and other
household bargains.

💲💲
NEW YORK CITY OPERA THRIFT SHOP

222 East 23rd Street, Gramercy Park 10010
212-684-5344
thriftshop@nycopera.com
www.nycopera.com
Mon-Fri 10:00-19:00; Sat 10:00-18:00;
Sun 12:00-17:00
Subway 6, N, R to 23rd Street

Perhaps the most attractive thrift shop in
the city, the spacious City Opera Thrift
Shop, at the head of East 23rd Street's
Thrift Row, features good quality men's
and women's clothing and accessories,
organized by color. We spotted cashmere
walking coats from Michael Kors
and Tahari, along with an Ann Taylor
pantsuit. New and nearly-new shoes are
neatly arranged on shelves. Browsing
the upstairs area is a pleasure, with
secondhand furniture, rugs and bric-a-
brac displayed in cozy vignettes. Furniture
included a shabby chic sideboard and
a red painted Shaker-style TV cabinet.
There's a good collection of opera and
classical music recordings on wax, along
with literature for the well-read. Proceeds
support the creation of costumes for the
New York City Opera at Lincoln Center.

💲
SALVATION ARMY FAMILY STORE

208 East 23rd Street, Gramercy Park 10010
212-532-8115
www.use.salvationarmy.org/gnyd
Mon-Sat 10:00-18:00 (Weds/Sat to 19:00)
Subway 6, N, R to 23rd Street

Like many who find their first job in
New York City, I relied on the Salvation
Army Store to furnish my apartment for a
pittance, and today's thrifty students scour
the racks for interesting pieces of clothing
to make their own. The international
religious and social organization, founded
in London in the 1860s, funds its adult
rehab centers through its sales of donated
merchandise. There are nine Salvation
Army Family Stores in Manhattan and
several more in the boroughs; the 23rd
Street shop sits on Gramercy's Thrift
Row and features a cheap and cheerful
array of clothing for the family, along with
linens, household goods, and furniture.
A big selection of televisions and audio
equipment was particularly notable.

$ $

VINTAGE THRIFT

286 Third Avenue, Gramercy Park 10010
212-871-7777
www.vintagethriftshop.org
Sun-Thu 11:00-19:00; Fri 10:30-dusk
(closed Sat)
Subway 6, N, R to 23rd Street

Founded in 2000, this tasteful and upscale
thrift shop benefits the United Jewish
Council of the East Side, which offers
a wide range of human services and
community development programs to
Manhattan's Lower East Side. Located
around the corner from Thrift Row, it is a
favorite of editors and bloggers with its
eclectic mix of clothing and accessories
(including designer names), jewelry,
furniture, art and antiques. Contemporary
and mid-century furniture is a strong suit
here, and the shop's artistically decorated
windows feature special pieces which are
sold via silent auction. Hours are adjusted
during the Jewish holidays, so do check
ahead.

Ⓢ
MONK THRIFT SHOP & DONATION CENTER

97 East Third Street, East Village 10003
212-673-7282
Mon-Sun 12:00-20:00
Subway 6 to Astor Place,
or F, M to Second Avenue

Not to be confused with Monk in Brooklyn (see p126), this large and cluttered shop is full of cheap secondhand clothes, ideal for starving artists and students. There's a big selection of T-shirts, flannels, and leather vests, along with the usual jeans, boots, trainers, hoodies, etc. Women's clothing includes some funky party clothes, and there's an interesting array of cameras, vintage toys, and over-the-top sunglasses. While no one in the shop could explain the "donation center" mentioned in the name, it's clear that the clothes and bric-a-brac have been donated; but the shop's beneficiary is not identified.

Ⓢ
EAST VILLAGE THRIFT SHOP

186 Second Avenue, East Village 10003
212-375-8585
Mon-Thu 10:00-21:00; Fri/Sat 10:00-22:00;
Sun 11:00-20:00
Subway L to Third Avenue or
First Avenue, or 6 to Astor Place

This shop gets terrific reviews from the locals for its "hidden gems" at downtown prices. Racks of donated clothing and accessories (mostly womenswear) require some patience to sort through, and while proceeds are said to benefit charitable organizations, the staff on hand could not give us further details. Short on atmosphere but long on bargains, this is destination shopping for below-14th Street's students and creative types.

LOWER EAST SIDE

$$

ECONOMY CANDY

108 Rivington Street, Lower East Side 10002
212-254-1531
economycandy@aol.com
www.economycandy.com
Mon 10:00-18:00; Tues-Fri/
Sun 09:00-18:00; Sat 10:00-17:00
Subway F, J, M, Z to Delancey & Essex Streets

While the merchandise is fresh, the ambiance at this old-fashioned neighborhood store couldn't be more vintage. Founded in 1937 in the midst of the Depression, the family-run shop is known as the "nosher's paradise of the Lower East Side." Bins of pick-and-mix include Bit-o-Honeys, Maryjanes, Tootsie Rolls, Smarties and the like. Giant Sugar Daddys, candy necklaces, wax lips, Moon Pies and Pop Rocks fill the shelves along with more sophisticated offerings such as imported chocolates, dried fruits and nuts, halvah and Turkish Delight. Collectors of Pez, the absurdly themed decorative dispensers of candy pellets, will find Disney characters and other rarities here. Economy Candy is a visual treat as well as a sugar rush.

$$$

ELEGANT WOOLEN AND SILK

74 Orchard Street, Lower East Side 10002
212-477-3443
Mon-Sun 11:00-19:00
Subway F, J, M, Z to Delancey & Essex Streets

The Lower East Side was once full of fabric shops like this, the legacy of the neighborhood's immigrant tailors and pushcart vendors. The narrow space is lined with shelves filled with owner Sammy Benzaken's collection of top-quality fabrics; some are 50 years old, such as vintage worsteds from Manchester and Huddlesfield. Flannels and tweeds, pinstripes and glen checks, Pima cotton shirtings and silk linings are lovingly measured out with an old-fashioned yardstick. Period costume designers shop here for "fabrics that are not made anymore," Sammy told us proudly. Like many of the small businesses in the Lower East Side, Elegant Woolen and Silk is under pressure from its landlord. "Maybe I'll move to Astoria," Sammy said resignedly.

$ $

BROOKLYN FLEA FORT GREENE

176 Lafayette Avenue, between Claremont and Vanderbilt Avenue, Fort Greene 11205
info@brooklynflea.com
www.brooklynflea.com
Sat 10:00-17:00 (April-Nov, rain or shine)
Subway G to Clinton-Washington Avenues

Founded in 2008, the original Brooklyn Flea features some 150 vendors of vintage and whimsical collectibles in the 40,000 square-foot schoolyard of Bishop Loughlin Memorial High School, on the border of the attractive family neighborhoods of Fort Greene and Clinton Hill. Papushka Village's dramatic ethnic pieces from the 60s stand out, along with their beautiful lace collars and lingerie, and classic leather goods such as Ferragamo boots and belts (www.papushka.com). Addicted to Vintage specializes in vinyl LPs, vintage guitars and other string instruments. Wrecords by Monkey (www.wrecordsbymonkey.com) rescues old records destined for landfill and transforms them into funky jewelry and art. Like many of New York's former specialty shops, Alphaville moved its

business to the Internet (www.alphaville. com) and the flea markets; the purveyor of toys, games and treasures from the 1950s has a wonderful collection of Milton Bradley board games, ViewMaster sets, and Warner Brothers cartoon character memorabilia. Past Diana's Vintage Bikes, a great array of vintage designer specs and shades at Extinct Optics (www. extinctoptics.com), and Hunters & Gatherers' taxidermy (a mini Museum of Natural History) are Brady & Kowalski's (www.brady-kowalski.com) curated selection of typewriters. We wanted to spend the afternoon lounging under the tent on Anthony Franck's beautiful antique rugs, some dating from the mid-19th century.

Anthony used to live in Turkey where he started collecting, and had an East Village shop for 15 years. "Most people don't know about rugs; color is everything," he told us. A Little of India is a home textiles and furniture collection using reclaimed, recycled and renewed materials designed by husband and wife team John and Avian Carraby, who were inspired by their visits to India. Foodies hold Brooklyn Flea in high esteem, with goodies such as fresh oysters from Brooklyn Fish Camp, homemade fruity ice pops from People's Pops, gourmet grilled cheese, lobster rolls, bubble tea and more.

WRECORDS BY MONKEY AT *BROOKLYN FLEA*

"ITS PRETTY STUPID WHAT YOU CAN DO WITH A GOOD IDEA."

Patrick Chirico (Monkey) and Brian Farrell handcraft their unique jewelry and interior products from reclaimed vinyl records, saving thousands of them from landfills. Their modestly-priced, upcycled wax bracelets, pendants, wall art and notebooks feature their energetic silk-screened graphics, and have been a big hit at Brooklyn Flea, as well as in art museums and boutiques in over 20 states.

The two started making their bracelets in 2004, and today operate out of a studio in Williamsburg, where they've handmade over 20,000 of their record bracelets. A graduate of New York's Fashion Institute of Technology, Monkey's interest in fashion came from his godmother, who taught him to sew. "A support system is important," says Monkey, who now mentors student artists in the process of silk-screening.

The duo also works on custom projects including graphic design, promotion, packaging and displays. "It's pretty stupid what you can do with a good idea," he muses. In his spare time, Monkey is making his fiancée's wedding gown.

$ $

FILM BIZ PROP SHOP

540 President Street, Gowanus 11215
347-384-2336
info@filmbizrecycling.org
www.filmbizrecycling.org
Mon-Fri 10:00-19:00; Sat/Sun 12:00-19:00
Subway R to Union Street, or 2, 3, 4, 5, B, D,
N, Q, R to Atlantic Avenue

This 11,000 square-foot basement warehouse is full of fascinating and useful secondhand items for sale or rent, culled from New York's television and film industry. Founded in 2008, Film Biz Recycling is a not-for-profit organization that places and repurposes used props, keeping tons of waste out of local landfill, with 60 percent of donated materials redistributed to local businesses or donated to shelters or local community foundations such as Materials for the Arts. Furniture and fabric, tools and typewriters, bicycles and bathtubs, cameras and curtains, period electronics and even buckets of paint are priced to sell; and there are collections of small props such as clocks, keys, hospital and religious paraphernalia, or holiday decorations that are sold "by the box." Film Biz is a great concept and is a great place to shop.

$ $

BROOKLYN FLEA SKYLIGHT ONE HANSON

1 Hanson Place, Fort Greene 11205
info@brooklynflea.com
www.brooklynflea.com
Sat/Sun 10:00-17:00 (Dec-March)
Subway 2, 3, 4, 5, B, D, N, Q, R
to Atlantic Avenue

Flea market addicts can come in from the cold during the winter months at Skylight One Hanson, where some 100 of Brooklyn Flea's vendors congregate on weekends. The landmark Art Deco building, the former Williamsburg Savings Bank, is worth seeing; and the Flea's gourmet food vendors are reason enough to make the trip.

$$

LIFE EMPORIUM

515 Fifth Avenue, Park Slope 11215
718-788-5433
Mon-Thu/Sun 11:00-18:00; Fri 11:00-17:00
Subway D, F, G, N, R to
Fourth Avenue/Ninth Street

This non-profit thrift store benefits Jewish children's charity Chai Lifeline, but the merchandise is a cut above your usual 'thrift' stuff and includes current designer finds for men and women, along with furniture, jewelry, sporting goods, and household knick-knacks. Set off by concrete floors and an industrial ambience – an Imperial flat-bed handknitting machine was among the items for sale – there are some great finds, such as an Alexander McQueen mesh vest and Ralph Lauren men's shirts, along with racks of pretty cocktail dresses. Women's shoes, curated by vintage stylist Zia Ziprin of Girls Love Shoes, take pride of place here.

$ $
MONK VINTAGE THRIFT SHOP

579 Fifth Avenue, Park Slope 11215
718-788-2950
Mon-Sat 11:00-20:00; Sun 11:00-19:00
Subway R to Prospect Avenue

It's hard to beat the prices at this funky, cluttered emporium of treasures and trash, but it's more secondhand than vintage. There are casual classics for men and women: polo shirts and mesh tees, cargos and beach shorts, jeans and shoes. We found an unworn wedding dress, along with a selection of secondhand contemporary separates and some slightly more outrageous outfits from the 1960s and 70s. The household bric-a-brac includes everything from games, records, CDs, books, cans of paint, and a wonderful Howdy Doody doll. Throw in an offbeat selection of neckties, jewelry, kids clothes, and handbags, for hours of browsing fun.

$ $
THE PARLOR SALE

313 Clinton Avenue, Clinton Hill 11205
Sat 10:00-17:00 (April-Sept)
Subway G to Clinton-Washington Avenues

Built in 1882 for lace manufacturer Albert Gould Jennings, this landmarked brownstone is also known as 'The Halloween House' for the over-the-top display put on by the owners every Halloween since 1994. The Parlor Sale is a collective offering of books, dolls, fabric and notions, shoes and clothes, and genteel bric-a-brac that attracts passers-by from Brooklyn Flea in Fort Greene. Reportedly haunted, the house and its parlor capture a bit of old-time Brooklyn ambience.

⑤⑤⑤

ARTISTS & FLEAS

70 North Seventh Street,
Williamsburg 11249
info@artistsandfleas.com
www.artistsandfleas.com
Sat/Sun 10:00-19:00
Subway L to Bedford Avenue,
or G to Metropolitan Avenue

This year-round, weekend 'retail alternative' in a 1930s warehouse just a block or so from Williamsburg's Brooklyn Flea is a love-in of emerging artists, indie designers, vintage collectors and crafters. Owners Amy Abrams and Ronen Glimer foster a sense of community and entrepreneurship among the vendors; while the mix changes weekly, some vendors are regulars. Gypsy Nation Vintage (www.gypsynationvintage.com) reflects owner Martha Camarillo's wanderlust with a collection of vintage caftans, gypsy skirts, handmade sandals and one-of-a-kind folkwear from far-flung places such as India, Uzbekistan, the Far East and western America. The Spooky Boutique specializes in "exceptional" vintage clothing, much of it couture, as well as menswear, shoes and accessories. Owner Ricky Becker also refashions some of his finds to create new from old. Another Work in Progress cleverly upcycles antique board and card games into diaries, bound books, spiral notebooks, storage boxes and clocks. The market becomes the Brooklyn Holiday Bazaar during the month of December; check for special opening hours.

$ $

BROOKLYN FLEA
WILLIAMSBURG

**East River Waterfront between North Sixth
and Seventh Streets,
North Williamsburg 11249
Info@brooklynflea.com
www.brooklynflea.com
Sun 10:00-17:00 (April-Nov, rain or shine)
Subway L to Bedford Avenue,
or East River Ferry to North Sixth Street**

Williamsburg's flea market offers a hipster's assortment of indie crafts, vintage finds, and trendy snacks, while the mix of vendors changes from week to week. Many are members of Etsy, the e-commerce site for artisans, crafters, vintage traders and upcyclers, who re-use and re-purpose old items to create new ones. The Etsy Vintage Pavilion features several vendors such as Max & Chichi, whose vintage basics include pretty cotton tanks and undies, along with funky 70s and 80s bathing suits. You can almost smell the chocolate chip cookies baking at Betty's Kitschen (www.bettyskitschen.etsy.com) where the charming collection of kitchenware, cookbooks, and 1950s aprons are modestly priced. At Fort (www.fort.etsy.com), delicate jewelry is hand-crafted from old or dead stock, and lovely notebooks are covered with wood veneer from architectural samples or leather from old upholstery. Recycled Relics (www.etsy.com/shop/RecycledRelics) uses architectural salvage to fashion home accents such as wooden and pressed tin frames, mirrors, bobbins and candlesticks. At Kasbah Moderne (www.kasbahmod.com) type enthusiast Chase Gilbert has amassed New York's largest collection of vintage typewriters, such as a Swiss Hermes 3000, all fully-functional and

many customized; along with vintage cameras including a 100-year-old Kodak and a more recent Kodak Duaflex II. With a nearby East Williamsburg workshop and warehouse (open by appointment, 917-701-5367), Retrogreen's vast inventory includes vintage eyeframes and bicycles, cameras and typewriters, as well as mid-century farm implements, suitcases, folk art, garden furniture and more. Proprietor Andre van Hoek's passion for the past is evident in the care given to curating and organizing his finds. Daily Memorandum's Zak and Alicia (www.dailymemorandum.com) are based in Philadelphia but spend weekends at Brooklyn Flea. Their motto, "an intellectual's Americana," is evident in their farmhouse antiques, mid-century kitchenware, taxidermy and medical ephemera. Don't leave Brooklyn Flea without sampling the eats: fried chicken and biscuits at King's Crumb, wonderful flatbreads at Saltie, and Sunday Gravy, the Brooklyn version of Bolognese.

The Friends from Dallas at Brooklyn Flea Williamsburg

The heat and humidity of a July Sunday in Brooklyn didn't seem to faze Sarah Stimson and Margaret Browne as they paused at Brooklyn Flea Williamsburg to share a raspberry lemonade and flatbread sandwich. Sarah is a communications major at Texas A&M and was spending the summer in Manhattan, interning in visual display at Anthropologie (a US retailer doing an ace job at translating vintage style into new apparel and home furnishings). Margaret studies English and creative writing at Trinity University, San Antonio, and was up for a visit. They come to Williamsburg "to shop and hang out" and especially love "the no-name furniture stores." The vintage scene in Dallas, their home town, is less well-known. "People in Dallas have vintage, but they don't know what they have – awesome finds, really cheap," explains Sarah. "People in NYC know what they have, and charge accordingly."

JUNK

197 North Ninth Street, Williamsburg 11211
212-260-1851
www.junk11211.com
Mon-Sun 09:00-21:00

The name of the store says it all – but one person's junk is another person's treasure, so if you're feeling lucky, dive into the piles of used furniture and luggage, records and CDs, old magazines and postcards, books, tableware, dolls and stuffed animals, and some very unique naïve art. Junk specializes in overstocks and never-used merchandise; you can rummage through boxes of candles, tubs of buttons and racks of costume jewelry, and even the occasional clothing manufacturer's overrun. While the shop's a bit dusty and scruffy, you won't find better bargains.

NEW YORK
MAPS

The following collection of maps will help you navigate your way around New York's secondhand and vintage shops and markets. Each corresponds to the zones used in the preceding chapters – Uptown Manhattan, Midtown West/Chelsea, Gramercy Park/Thrift Row, East Village/NoHo/Greenwich Village, SoHo/Nolita/Tribeca, Lower East Side, Downtown Brooklyn and Williamsburg, Brooklyn.

Each entry is listed under its category and the color of the icon on the map corresponds to that category, with sites marked by diamonds:

CLOTHES AND ACCESSORIES

BOOKS, MUSIC & MEMORABILIA

HOME & INTERIORS

ONLY IN NEW YORK

A SELECT HANDFUL OF CAFES ARE MARKED BY A

Each map has a QR code. If you have a smartphone, you can simply scan the code to link to online versions of the maps on Google which will help you find your way around. These maps are regularly updated to keep pace with New York's evolving secondhand and vintage landscape.

UPTOWN MANHATTAN

CLOTHES ◆
BOOKS & MUSIC ◆
HOME & INTERIORS ◆
ONLY IN NEW YORK ◆

CLOTHES

1 A SECOND CHANCE
1109 Lexington Avenue
Mon-Fri 11:00-19:00
Sat 11:00-18:00

2 BIS DESIGNER RESALE
1134 Madison Avenue
Mon-Sat 10:00-18:00
(Thu to 19:00)
Sun 12:00-17:00

3 ENCORE
1132 Madison Avenue
Mon-Sat 10:30-18:30
(Thu to 19:30)
Sun 12:00-18:00

4 LA BOUTIQUE RESALE
1045 Madison Avenue
Mon-Sat 10:30-19:00
Sun 11:00-18:30

5 MICHAEL'S
1041 Madison Avenue
Mon-Sat 9:30-18:00
(Thu to 20:00)
(Sun closed; Sat/
Sun in July/Aug closed)

ONLY IN NEW YORK

6 ARTHRITIS FOUNDATION THRIFT SHOP
1430 Third Avenue
Mon-Sat 10:00-18:00
Sun 12:00-17:00

7 CANCER*CARE* THRIFT SHOP
1480 Third Avenue
Mon/Tues/Fri 11:00-18:00
Wed/Thu 11:00-19:00
Sat 11:00-16:30; Sun 12:30-17.00

8 COUNCIL THRIFT SHOP
246 East 84th Street
Mon-Thu 11:00-17:45
(Thu 11:00 to 19:45)
Fri/Sat 11:00-16:45

9 GREENFLEA
Columbus Avenue and
West 77th Street
Sun 10:00-17:45

10 MEMORIAL SLOANE-KETTERING THRIFT SHOP
1440 Third Avenue
Mon-Wed 10:00-17:30
Thu 10:00-18:00
Sat 11:00-17:00; Sun 12:00-17:00

11 SPENCE-CHAPIN THRIFT SHOP
1473 Third Avenue
Mon-Fri 11:00-18:00
Sat 11:00-17:00
Sun 12:00-17:00

FOOD & DRINK

12 ALICE'S TEA CUP
102 West 73rd Street
Mon-Sun 08:00-20:00

13 ALICE'S TEA CUP
220 East 81st Street
Mon-Sun 08:00-20:00

14 LE PAIN QUOTIDIEN
1131 Madison Avenue
Mon-Fri 07:00-19:30
Sat/Sun 08:00-19:30

15 LE PAIN QUOTIDIEN
50 West 72nd Street
Mon-Fri 07:00-19:30
Sat/Sun 08:00-19:30

16 LE PAIN QUOTIDIEN
252 East 77th Street
Mon-Fri 07:00-19:30
Sat/Sun 08:00-19:30

17 MAGNOLIA BAKERY
200 Columbus Avenue
Mon-Thu 07:30-22:00
Fri/Sat 07:30-00:30
Sun 07:30-22:00

MIDTOWN WEST/CHELSEA

CLOTHES ◆
BOOKS & MUSIC ◆
HOME & INTERIORS ◆
ONLY IN NEW YORK ◆

CLOTHES

1 BUFFALO EXCHANGE
114 West 26th Street
Mon-Sat 11:00-20:00
Sun 12:00-19:00

2 THE FAMILY JEWELS
130 West 23rd Street
Mon-Sun 11:00-19:00

3 FISCH FOR THE HIP
153 West 18th Street
Mon-Sat 12:00-19:00
Sun 12:00-18:00

4 PIPPIN VINTAGE JEWELRY
112 West 17th Street
Mon-Sat 11:00-19:00
Sun 12:00-18:00

5 REMINISCENCE
50 West 23rd Street
Mon-Sat 11:00-19:30
Sun 12:00-19:00

6 RITZ FURS
345 Seventh Avenue
Mon-Sat 10:00-17:30
(Sat in July closed; Aug closed)

7 SHAREEN VINTAGE
13 West 17th Street
Wed-Fri 13:00-21:00
Sat 14:00-18:00
(or by appointment)

BOOKS & MUSIC

8 30TH STREET GUITARS
236 West 30th Street
Mon-Fri 11:00-18:00 (Thu to 20:00)
Sat 11:00-17:00

9 ACADEMY RECORDS & CDS
12 West 18th Street
Sun-Wed 11:00-19:00
Thu-Sat 11:00-20:00

10 CHELSEA GUITARS
224 West 23rd Street
Mon-Sun 11:00-19:00

11 COLONY RECORDS
1619 Broadway
Mon-Sat 09:00-01:00
Sun 10:00-00:00

12 MANTIQUES MODERN
146 West 22nd Street
Mon-Fri 10:30-18:30
Sat/Sun 11:00-19:00

13 PERRY RITTER
71 West 47th Street
Mon-Fri 06:00-17:00

14 ROGUE MUSIC
220 West 30th Street
Mon/Sat 11:00-18:00
Tues-Fri 11:00-20:00

HOME & INTERIORS

15 NEW YORK GALLERIES ANTIQUES
111 West 25th Street
Mon-Sun 10:00-18:00

16 OLDE GOOD THINGS
124 West 24th Street
Mon-Sun 10:00-19:00

17 PIPPIN VINTAGE HOME
112½ West 17th Street
Mon-Sat 10:00-19:00
Sun 12:00-18:00

18 SECONDHAND ROSE
230 Fifth Avenue
Mon-Fri 10:00-18:00

ONLY IN NEW YORK

19 **B&J FABRICS**
525 Seventh Avenue
Mon-Fri 08:00-17:45
Sat 09:00-16:45

20 **THE GARAGE ANTIQUE FLEA MARKET**
112 West 25th Street
Sat/Sun 09:00-17:00

21 **HELL'S KITCHEN FLEA MARKET**
West 39th Street, between Ninth
and Tenth Avenues
Sat/Sun 09:00-18:00
(weather permitting)

22 **HOUSING WORKS**
143 West 17th Street
Mon-Fri 10:00-19:00
Sat 10:00-18:00
Sun 12:00-17:00

23 **HYMAN HENDLER & SONS**
21 West 38th Street
Mon-Fri 09:00-17:00

24 **NEW YORK DIAMOND DISTRICT**
West 47th Street, between Fifth and
Sixth Avenues
Check individual stores for hours;
many open every day

25 **ROSEN & CHADICK FABRICS**
561 Seventh Avenue
Mon-Fri 8:30-17:45; Sat 09:00-16:30

26 **SHOWPLACE DESIGN + ANTIQUE CENTER**
40 West 25th Street
Mon-Fri 10:00-18:00
Sat/Sun 08:30-15:30

27 **TINSEL TRADING COMPANY**
1 West 37th Street
Mon-Fri 09:45-18:00
Sat 11:00-17:00

28 **WEST 25TH STREET MARKET**
29-37 West 25th Street
Sat/Sun 09:00-17:00

FOOD & DRINK

29 **ARGO TEA CAFÉ**
275 Seventh Avenue
Mon-Fri 06:00-23:00
Sat 07:00-23:00
Sun 07:00-22:00

30 **CHELSEA MARKET**
75 Ninth Avenue
Mon-Sat 07:00-21:00
Sun 08:00-20:00

31 **LA MAISON DU MACARON**
132 West 23rd Street
Mon-Fri 07:00-20:00
Sat/Sun 08:00-20:00

32 **THE DOUGHNUT PLANT**
220 West 23rd Street
Mon-Fri 07:00-22:00
Sat/Sun 08:00-22:00

GRAMERCY PARK/
THRIFT ROW

CLOTHES ◆
BOOKS & MUSIC ◆
HOME & INTERIORS ◆
ONLY IN NEW YORK ◆

East 25th Street

East 24th Street

Ⓜ 23 St
400m walk

2nd Avenue

East 22nd Street

⑤

East 23rd Street

④ ④ ② ③ ①

Ⓜ 14 St - Union Sq
approx. 500m walk

East 21st Street

East 20th Street

1000ft
200m

⑥

Ⓜ 3 Av
approx. 500m walk

ONLY IN NEW YORK

CAUZ FOR PAWZ
212 East 23rd Street
Mon-Sat 10:00-19:30
Sun 11:00-18:00

GOODWILL STORE
220 East 23rd Street
Mon-Sat 10:00-20:00
Sun 10:00-19:00

NEW YORK CITY OPERA THRIFT STORE
222 East 23rd Street
Mon-Fri 10:00-19:00
Sat 10:00-18:00; Sun 12:00-17:00

SALVATION ARMY FAMILY STORE
208 East 23rd Street
Mon-Sat 10:00-18:00
(Wed/Sat to 19:00)

VINTAGE THRIFT
286 Third Avenue
Sun-Thu 11:00-19:00
Fri 10:30-dusk
(closed Sat)

FOOD & DRINK

ESS-A-BAGEL
359 First Avenue
Mon-Sat 06:00-21:00
Sun 06:00-17:00

JESS BAKERY
221 East 23rd Street
Mon-Fri 07:30-22:00
Sat/Sun 09:30-21:00

EAST VILLAGE/NOHO/ GREENWICH VILLAGE

CLOTHES ◆
BOOKS & MUSIC ◆
HOME & INTERIORS ◆
ONLY IN NEW YORK ◆

CLOTHES

1 ANGELA'S VINTAGE BOUTIQUE
330 East 11th Street
Mon-Sun 12:00-20:00

2 AUH₂O THRIFTIQUE
84 East Seventh Street
Mon-Sun 12:00-20:00

3 BEST OF RYLEY INC
345 Lafayette
Mon-Fri 10:00-20:00
Sat/Sun 11:00-20:00

4 CADILLAC'S CASTLE
333 East Ninth Street
Mon-Sun 12:00-20:00

5 COBBLESTONES
314 East Ninth Street
Tues-Sun 13:00-19:00

6 DUO
227 East Ninth Street
Mon-Sun 12:30-20:30

7 DUSTY BUTTONS
441 East Ninth Street
Tues-Fri 12:00-20:00
Sat 12:00-19:00; Sun 12:00-18:00

8 ELEVEN CONSIGNMENT BOUTIQUE
180 First Avenue
Mon-Wed 10:00-22:00
Thu-Sat 10:00-23:00
Sun 11:00-20:00

9 FABULOUS FANNY'S
335 East Ninth Street
Mon-Sun 12:00-20:00

10 LADIES & GENTLEMEN
338 East 11th Street
Mon-Sun 13:00-20:00

11 LIMITED SUPPLY
273 East Tenth Street
Mon-Sun 11:00-20:00

12 MATIELL
350 East Ninth Street
Mon-Sun 12:30-20:00

13 MINA
32A Cooper Square
Mon-Sat 11:00-19:00; Sun 12:00-18:00

14 NO RELATION VINTAGE
204 First Avenue
Mon-Thu 13:00-20:00
Fri 13:00-21:00; Sat 12:00-21:00
Sun 12:00-20:00

15 REASON OUTPOST
436 East Ninth Street
Mon-Sun 12:00-20:00

16 RENA REBORN
117 East Seventh Street
Mon-Sat 11:00-20:00/Sun 12:00-18:00

17 RUE ST. DENIS
170 Avenue B
Mon-Fri 12:00-20:00
Sat/Sun 12:00-19:00

18 SCREAMING MIMI'S
382 Lafayette Street
Mon-Sat 12:00-20:00; Sun 13:00-19:00

19 STOCK VINTAGE
143 East 13th Street
Mon-Fri 12:00-20:00
Sat 12:00-19:00; Sun 12:00-18:00

20 TOKIO7
83 East Seventh Street
Mon-Sun 12:00-20:00

21 TOKYO JOE
334 East 11th Street
Mon-Sun 12:00-21:00

22 VILLAGE STYLE
111 East Seventh Street
Mon-Thu 13:00-21:00
Fri-Sat 12:00-22:00; Sun 12:00-20:00

23 VOZ
618 East Ninth Street
Mon-Sat 12:00-19:00
Sun 12:00-18:00

BOOKS & MUSIC

24 **ARCHANGEL ANTIQUES**
334 East Ninth Street
Wed-Sat 15:00-19:00

25 **BONNIE SLOTNICK COOKBOOKS**
163 West Tenth Street
Most days 13:00-19:00

26 **EAST VILLAGE BOOKS**
99 St. Mark's Place
Mon-Thu 13:00-23:00
Fri 13:00-00:00
Sat 12:00-23:00; Sun 13:00-21:00

27 **EAST VILLAGE MUSIC STORE**
21 East Third Street
Mon-Fri 12:00-20:00
Sat 14:00-20:00

28 **KABINETT & KAMMER**
174 East Second Street
Wed-Sat 12:00-20:00
Sun 12:00-17:00

29 **SPIRIT AND MATTER**
180 East Tenth Street
Mon-Sun 15:00-19:00

30 **STRAND BOOK STORE**
828 Broadway
Mon-Sat 09:30-22:30
Sun 11:00-22:30

HOME & INTERIORS

31 **LANDMARK VINTAGE BICYCLES**
136 East Third Street
Mon-Fri 11:00-20:00
Sat/Sun 11:00-18:00

32 **LOST CITY ARTS**
18 Cooper Square
Mon-Fri 10:00-18:00
Sat/Sun 12:00-18:00

33 **RECYCLE-A-BICYCLE**
75 Avenue C
Mon-Sat 12:00-19:00
Sun 12:00-17:00

34 **THE UPPER RUST**
445 East Ninth Street
Wed-Mon 12:00-19:00

ONLY IN NEW YORK

35 **EAST VILLAGE THRIFT SHOP**
186 Second Avenue
Mon-Thu 10:00-21:00
Fri/Sat 10:00-22:00
Sun 11:00-20:00

36 **MONK THRIFT SHOP & DONATION CENTER**
97 East Third Street
Mon-Sun 12:00-20:00

FOOD & DRINK

37 **BUTTER LANE**
123 East Seventh Street
Mon/Sun 11:00-22:00
Tues-Thu 11:00-23:00
Fri/Sat 11:00-00:00

38 **MUD COFFEE**
307 East Ninth Street
Mon-Fri 08:00-12:00
Sat/Sun 09:00-12:00

39 **VENIERO PASTICCIERIA**
342 East 11th Street
Mon-Thu/Sun 08:00-00:00
Fri/Sat 08:00-1:00

SOHO/NOLITA/TRIBECA

CLOTHES ◆
BOOKS & MUSIC ◆
HOME & INTERIORS ◆
ONLY IN NEW YORK ◆

Greenwich Village

Soho

Little Italy

Chinatown

Tribeca

500ft
200m

CLOTHES

1 THE CLOTHING WAREHOUSE
8 Prince Street
Mon-Thu 11:30-19:00
Fri/Sat 11:30-20:00; Sun 12:00-19:00

2 FREITAG
1 Prince Street
Tues-Sun 11:00-19:00
(Thu to 21:00)

3 INA
19 and 21 Prince Street
Mon-Sat 12:00-20:00
Sun 12:00-19:00

4 MARMALADE VINTAGE
174 Mott Street
Mon-Sun 13:00-19:00

5 THE QUALITY MENDING CO.
15 Prince Street
Mon-Sat 12:00-20:00
Sun 12:00-19:00

6 REBORN PROCESS
35 Crosby Street
Mon-Wed 12:00-19:00
Thu-Sat 11:00-19:00
Sun 12:00-18:00

7 RESURRECTION
217 Mott Street
Mon-Sat 11:00-19:00
Sun 12:00-19:00

8 RITUAL VINTAGE
377 Broome Street
Mon-Sun 12:00-20:00

**9 WHAT GOES AROUND
COMES AROUND**
351 West Broadway
Mon-Sat 11:00-20:00
Sun 12:00-19:00

HOME & INTERIORS

16 OCHRE
462 Broome Street
Mon-Sat 11:00-19:00
Sun 12:00-18:00

BOOKS & MUSIC

10 FOUNTAIN PEN HOSPITAL
10 Warren Street
Mon-Fri 07:30-17:30

11 HOUSING WORKS BOOKSTORE CAFÉ
126 Crosby Street
Mon-Fri 10:00-21:00
Sat/Sun 10:00-17:00

12 THE MYSTERIOUS BOOKSHOP
58 Warren Street
Mon-Sat 11:00-19:00

13 PHILLIP WILLIAMS POSTERS
122 Chambers Street
Mon-Sat 11:00-19:00
(Mon in July/Aug closed)

14 WORKING CLASS
168 Duane Street
Mon-Sun 11:00-19:00

15 WRK DESIGN
32 Prince Street
Mon-Sun 11:00-19:00

FOOD & DRINK

17 BUBBY'S
120 Hudson Street
Tues-Sun open 24 hours
(Mon open till 00:00)

18 CAFÉ GITANE
242 Mott Street
Mon-Thu/Sun 08:30-00:00
Fri-Sat 08:30-00:30

19 THE GREY DOG
244 Mulberry Street
Mon-Fri 06:30-23:30
Sat/Sun 07:00-23:30

20 KITCHENETTE
156 Chambers Street
Mon-Fri 07:00-23:00
Sat/Sun 09:00-23:00

21 LITTLE CUPCAKE BAKESHOP
30 Prince Street
Mon-Fri 07:00-23:00
Sat/Sun 08:00-23:00

LOWER EAST SIDE

CLOTHES ◆
BOOKS & MUSIC ◆
HOME & INTERIORS ◆
ONLY IN NEW YORK ◆

East 3rd Street

East 1st Street

13 Ⓜ 2 Av

East Houston Street

Stanton Street

Stanton Street

Allen Street

Chrystie Street

12

Rivington Street

10

3

9

1

Forsyth Street

2 4 7

6

The Bowery

Ⓜ Bowery

Essex St

Stanton St

Norfolk Street

Suffolk Street

9

Delancey Street

Rivington Street

5

ome Street

Eldridge Street

Ⓜ Delancey & Essex St

11

Orchard Street

Ⓜ Grand St

Ludlow Street

Broome Street

Norfolk Street

Suffolk Street

ystie Street

Forsyth Street

Grand Street

200ft

100m

Allen Street

14

Essex St

Clinton Street

Hester Street

Lower East

CLOTHES

1 A. TUREN
85 Stanton Street
Tues-Sat 12:00-20:00
Sun 12:00-19:00

2 ANY OLD IRON
149 Orchard Street
Sun-Wed 12:00-19:00
Thu-Sat 12:00-20:00

3 ASSEMBLY NEW YORK
170 Ludlow Street
Mon-Sun 12:00-21:00

4 DAVID OWENS VINTAGE CLOTHING
154 Orchard Street
Mon-Sun 12:00-20:00

5 MOSCOT
118 Orchard Street
Mon-Fri 10:00-19:00
Sat 10:30-18:00; Sun 12:00-18:00

6 THE REFORMATION
156 Ludlow Street
Mon-Sat 12:00-20:00
Sun 12:00-19:00

7 SOME ODD RUBIES
151 Ludlow Street
Mon-Fri 13:00-20:00
Sat 12:00-20:00; Sun 12:00-19:00

HOME & INTERIORS

8 LAS VENUS
163 Ludlow Street
Mon-Fri 11:00-19:00
Sat/Sun 12:00-19:00

ONLY IN NEW YORK

9 ECONOMY CANDY
108 Rivington Street
Mon 10:00-18:00
Tues-Fri/Sun 09:00-18:00
Sat 10:00-17:00

10 ELEGANT WOOLEN AND SILK
174 Orchard Street
Mon-Sun 11:00-19:00

FOOD & DRINK

11 IL LABORATORIO DEL GELATO
95 Orchard Street
Mon-Thu 07:30-00:00
Fri 07:30-00:00; Sat 10:00-00:00
Sun 10:00-22:00

12 KATZ'S DELICATESSEN
205 East Houston Street
Mon-Wed 08:00-22:45
Thu 08:00-02:45
Fri 08:00 till Sun 22:45

13 YONAH SHIMMEL'S KNISHES
137 East Houston Street
Mon-Thu 09:00-19:30
Fri-Sat 09:00-23:00
Sun 09:00-19:00

14 THE PICKLE GUYS
49 Essex Street
Mon-Thu/Sun 09:00-18:00
Fri 09:00-16:00

DOWNTOWN BROOKLYN

CLOTHES ◆
BOOKS & MUSIC ◆
HOME & INTERIORS ◆
ONLY IN NEW YORK ◆

CLOTHES

1 EPONYMY
466 Bergen Street
Tues-Fri 12:00-19:00
Sat 11:00-19:00; Sun 12:00-18:00

2 EVA GENTRY CONSIGNMENT
371 Atlantic Avenue
Mon-Sat 12:00-19:00
Sun 12:00-18:00

3 GUVNOR'S VINTAGE THRIFT
178 Fifth Avenue
Sun-Wed 12:00-19:30
Thu/Fri 12:00-20:00
Sat 11:00-20:00

4 ODD TWIN
164 Fifth Avenue
Mon-Fri 12:00-20:00
Sat/Sun 11:00-20:00

5 OLAF'S MEN'S VINTAGE
453 Court Street
Mon-Fri 12:00-20:00
Sat 11:00-21:00; Sun 11:00-18:00

6 OLIVE'S VERY VINTAGE
434 Court Street
Mon-Fri 12:00-20:00
Sat 11:00-20:00; Sun 10:00-18:00

7 PONY
69 Fifth Avenue
Mon-Sat 12:00-20:00
Sun 12:00-19:00

8 SMITH + BUTLER
225 Smith Street
Mon 12:00-19:00
Tues/Wed 12:00-19:30
Thu-Sat 11:00-19:30; Sun 12:00-18:00

BOOKS & MUSIC

9 BROWNSTONE TREASURES
220 Court Street
Tues-Sun 11:00-18:00

10 THE COMMUNITY BOOKSTORE
212 Court Street
Mon-Sun 15:00-23:00
(Aug/Sept closed)

11 DARR
369 Atlantic Avenue
Mon-Sat 11:00-19:00
Sun 12:00-18:00

12 FORK + PENCIL
221a Court Street
Tues-Sun 11:00-19:00

13 RETROFRET/MUSURGIA
233 Butler Street
Mon-Fri 12:00-19:00; Sat 12:00-18:00

14 STERLING PLACE
363 Atlantic Avenue
Mon-Fri 11:00-18:30
Sat 11:00-19:00; Sun 12:00-18:00

15 VINTAGE SIGNAGE
334 Atlantic Avenue
Mon-Sun 11:30-19:00

HOME & INTERIORS

16 CIRCA ANTIQUES
374 Atlantic Avenue
Tues-Sat 11:00-18:00; Sun 12:00-18:00

17 CITY FOUNDRY
365 Atlantic Avenue
Tues-Thu (by appointment)
Fri-Sun 11:00-19:00

18 HORSEMAN ANTIQUES
351 Atlantic Avenue
Mon-Fri 10:00-19:00; Sat 11:00-19:00
Sun 12:00-19:00

19 TIME GALLERIES
562 Fifth Avenue
Mon-Sat 09:00-18:00
Sun 12:00-18:00

ONLY IN NEW YORK

20 BROOKLYN FLEA FORT GREENE
176 Lafayette Avenue
Sat 10:00-17:00
(April-Nov, rain or shine)

21 BROOKLYN FLEA SKYLIGHT ONE HANSON
1 Hanson Place
Sat/Sun 10:00-17:00 (Dec-March)

22 FILM BIZ PROP SHOP
540 President Street
Mon-Fri 10:00-19:00
Sat/Sun 12:00-19:00

23 LIFE EMPORIUM
515 Fifth Avenue
Mon-Thu/Sun 11:00-18:00
Fri 11:00-17:00

24 MONK VINTAGE THRIFT SHOP
579 Fifth Avenue
Mon-Sat 11:00-20:00
Sun 11:00-19:00

25 THE PARLOR SALE
313 Clinton Avenue
Sat 10:00-17:00 (April-Sept)

FOOD & DRINK

26 THE CHOCOLATE ROOM
86 Fifth Avenue
Mon-Thu/Sun 12:00-23:00
Fri-Sat 12:00-00:00

27 GORILLA COFFEE
97 Fifth Avenue
Mon-Sat 07:00-21:00
Sun 08:00-21:00

28 THE MARQUET PATISSERIE
221 Court Street
Mon-Fri 07:00-20:00
Sat/Sun 08:00-20:00

29 NAIDRE'S
384 Seventh Avenue
Mon-Sun 07:00-20:00

30 NUNU
529 Atlantic Avenue
Mon-Fri 07:00-21:00
Sat/Sun 09:00-21:00

31 SAHADI'S
187 Atlantic Avenue
Mon-Fri 09:00-19:00
Sat 09:00-18:00

WILLIAMSBURG
BROOKLYN

CLOTHES ◆
BOOKS & MUSIC ◆
HOME & INTERIORS ◆
ONLY IN NEW YORK ◆

North 12th Street

North 15th

North 12th

North 11th S

North 10th Stre

North 9th Street

North 8th Street

North 7th Street

North 7th Street

North 5th Street

3rd Street

Kent Avenue

Wythe Street

Berry Street

Bedford Avenue

M Bedford Av

North 6th Street

North 5th Street

North 4th Street

North 3rd Street

North 1st Street

Driggs Avenue

Grand Street

Fillmore Place

South 1st

Street

3

10

12

9

5

7

1
15
8
14

13
2

6

4

200ft
100m

Lorimer St
approx.
400m walk
M

CLOTHES

ABOUT GLAMOUR
107A North Third Street
Sun-Thu 12:00-20:00
Fri 12:00-21:00; Sat 12:00-22:00

AMARCORD VINTAGE FASHION
223 Bedford Avenue
Mon-Sun 12:00-20:00

BEACON'S CLOSET
88 North 11th Street
Mon-Fri 11:00-21:00
Sat/Sun 11:00-20:00

LE GRAND STRIP
197 Grand Street
Mon-Sat 12:00-20:00
Sun 12:00-19:00

MALIN LANDAEUS
155 North Sixth Street
Sun-Thu 11:00-21:00
Fri/Sat 11:00-22:30

VICE VERSA
241 Bedford Avenue
Mon-Thu 13:00-20:00
Fri/Sat 12:00-22:00; Sun 12:00-20:00

BOOKS & MUSIC

UGLY LUGGAGE
214 Bedford Avenue
Mon-Fri 13:00-20:00
Sat/Sun 12:00-19:00

HOME & INTERIORS

**SANFORD AND SVEN'S
SECOND HAND**
106 North Third Street
Tues-Sun 13:00-19:30

ONLY IN NEW YORK

ARTISTS & FLEAS
70 North Seventh Street
Sat/Sun 10:00-19:00

BROOKLYN FLEA WILLIAMSBURG
East River Waterfront, between
North Sixth and Seventh Streets
Sun 10:00-17:00 (April-Nov, rain or
shine)

JUNK
197 North Ninth Street
Mon-Sun 9:00-21:00

FOOD & DRINK

BAKERI
150 Wythe Avenue
Mon-Sun 08:00-19:00

BEDFORD CHEESE SHOP
141 North Fourth Street
Mon-Fri 11:00-21:00
Sat 10:00-09:00; Sun 10:00-20:00

**MAST BROTHERS
CHOCOLATE FACTORY**
111 North Third Street
Mon-Sun 12:00-19:00

RADEGAST HALL & BIERGARTEN
113 North Third Street
Mon-Fri 16:00-04:00
Sat/Sun 12:00-04:00

NEW YORK
INDEX OF SHOPS

ACKNOWLEDGEMENTS

The author wishes to thank Lee Ripley, Andrew Whittaker, and the editing team at Vivays Publishing for their support. Additional thanks go to Tristine Berry, Nancy Daugherty, and Jennifer Sabatelle for their hospitality during my research.

I am extremely grateful to my photographers for their good-natured companionship and knowledge of New York's neighborhoods: Aba Gyepi-Garbrah, Ryan Scammell, Peter H. Tooker and Claudia D. Ward.

Thank you to the many shop owners and managers who so graciously shared their stories and allowed us to photograph their stores, and a special mention to the shopkeepers and shoppers who granted us interviews: Margaret Browne, Edward Capolongo, Patrick Chirico, Ayshe and Aylin Erinc, Kathryn Gardner, Stacy Iannacone, Naoko Ito, Scott Jordan, Malin Landaeus, Sarah Stimson, Ed Sullivan, Jennifer Toledo, Rex Wang and Christopher Zelasko.

Thank you as well to the following stores and their photographers who supplied press photos:

Meryl Friedman at Housing Works, photos by Julie Turkewitz.
Lisa Haspel at Vintage Thrift.
Hannah Kurland at Marmalade Vintage.
Jennifer McCulloch at Olive's Very Vintage, photos by Reuben Negrón.
Andrea Miller at Eponymy, photos by Gigi Gatewood and Samuel Morgan.
Carrie Peterson at Beacon's Closet.
Keith Tauber at Ritz Furs.

PHOTO CREDITS

p.4 Ryan Scammell; p.6 (left) Ryan Scammell, (right) Aba Gyepi-Garbrah; p.7 Ryan Scammell; p.8 (top/bottom) Aba Gyepi-Garbrah, (centre) Peter H. Tooker & Claudia D. Ward; p.9 (left/right) Aba Gyepi-Garbrah; p.10 Ryan Scammell; p.11 Ryan Scammell; p.12 (top/bottom) Aba Gyepi-Garbrah; p.13 (left/right) Aba Gyepi-Garbrah; p.14 (top/bottom) Aba Gyepi-Garbrah; p.15 Aba Gyepi-Garbrah; p.16 (left/right) Aba Gyepi-Garbrah; p.17 Aba Gyepi-Garbrah; p.18 (left) courtesy Keith Tauber; (right) Aba Gyepi-Garbrah; p.19 (top/bottom) Peter H. Tooker & Claudia D. Ward; p.20 (left) Aba Gyepi-Garbrah; (right) Peter H. Tooker & Claudia D. Ward; p.21 Aba Gyepi-Garbrah; p.22 (left/right) Peter H. Tooker & Claudia D. Ward; p.23 (left/right) Peter H. Tooker & Claudia D. Ward; p.24 (top/bottom) Peter H. Tooker & Claudia D. Ward; p.25 (top/bottom) Peter H. Tooker & Claudia D. Ward; p.26 Peter H. Tooker & Claudia D. Ward; p.27 (top) Peter H. Tooker & Claudia D. Ward, (bottom) Aba Gyepi-Garbrah; p. 28 Peter H. Tooker & Claudia D. Ward; p.29 (left/right) Peter H. Tooker & Claudia D. Ward; p.30 (left/right) Peter H. Tooker & Claudia D. Ward; p.31 (left) Aba Gyepi-Garbrah, (right) Peter H. Tooker & Claudia D. Ward; p.32 (left/right) Peter H. Tooker & Claudia D. Ward; p.33 (top/bottom) Peter H. Tooker & Claudia D. Ward; p.34 (top/bottom) Peter H. Tooker & Claudia D. Ward; p.35 Peter H. Tooker & Claudia D. Ward; p.36 (left/right) Ryan Scammell; p.37 courtesy Hannah Kurland; p.38 (left/right) Ryan Scammell; p.39 (left/right) Ryan Scammell; p.40 Ryan Scammell; p.41 Ryan Scammell; p.42 Ryan Scammell; p.43 (top/bottom) Ryan Scammell; p.44 (left/centre/right) Ryan Scammell; p.45 (left/right) Ryan Scammell; p.46 (top/bottom) Ryan Scammell; p.47 Ryan Scammell; p.48 (left) G.G Gatewood, courtesy Andrea Miller, (right) Ryan Scammell; p.49 Ryan Scammell; p.50 Reuben Negrón, courtesy Jennifer McCulloch; p.51 Ryan Scammell; p.52 Aba Gyepi-Garbrah; p.53 (top) Aba Gyepi-Garbrah; (bottom) courtesy Carrie Peterson; p.54 Aba Gyepi-Garbrah; p.55 (top/bottom) Aba Gyepi-Garbrah; p.57 (top/bottom) Aba Gyepi-Garbrah; p.58 Ryan Scammell; p.59 (top/bottom) Ryan Scammell; p.60 (left) Ryan Scammell, (right) Aba Gyepi-Garbrah; p.61 (top/bottom) Aba Gyepi-Garbrah; p.62 (left) Debra Johnston Cobb, (right) Ryan Scammell; p.63 Debra Johnston Cobb; p.64 Ryan Scammell; p.62 (top/bottom) Ryan Scammell; p.67 (top/bottom) Peter H. Tooker & Claudia D. Ward; p.68 (left/right) Ryan Scammell; p.69 Peter H. Tooker & Claudia D. Ward; p.70 (left/right) Peter H. Tooker & Claudia D. Ward; p.71 Peter H. Tooker & Claudia D. Ward; p.72 Ryan Scammell; p.73 Ryan Scammell; p.74 Julie Turkewitz, courtesy Meryl Friedman; p.75 Ryan Scammell; p.76 (top/bottom) Ryan Scammell; p.77 Ryan Scammell; p.78 (top/bottom) Aba Gyepi-Garbrah; p.79 (left) Ryan Scammell, (right) Aba Gyepi-Garbrah; p.80 (left) Ryan Scammell, (right) Aba Gyepi-Garbrah; p.81 Ryan Scammell; p.82 (left/right) Ryan Scammell; p.83 Aba Gyepi-Garbrah; p.84 Ryan Scammell; p.85 (left/right) Ryan Scammell; p.86 Aba Gyepi-Garbrah; p.87 (left) Aba Gyepi-Garbrah, (right) Ryan Scammell; p.88 (top) Aba Gyepi-Garbrah, (left/right) Peter H. Tooker & Claudia D. Ward; p.89 Peter H. Tooker & Claudia D. Ward; p.90 Aba Gyepi-Garbrah; p.91 (top/bottom) Ryan Scammell; p.92-93 (top/centre/bottom) Ryan Scammell; p.94 (left/right) Ryan Scammell; p.95 Aba Gyepi-Garbrah; p.96 Aba Gyepi-Garbrah; p.97 Peter H. Tooker & Claudia D. Ward; p.98 Aba Gyepi-Garbrah; p.99 Aba Gyepi-Garbrah; p.100 (left/right) Aba Gyepi-Garbrah; p.101 Aba Gyepi-Garbrah; p.102 Aba Gyepi-Garbrah; p.104 Aba Gyepi-Garbrah; p.105 Aba Gyepi-Garbrah; p.106 Debra Johnston Cobb; p.107 (left/right) Aba Gyepi-Garbrah; p.108 (left/right) Aba Gyepi-Garbrah; p.109 (top/bottom) Aba Gyepi-Garbrah; p.110 (top) Julie Turkewitz courtesy Meryl Friedman, (bottom) Debra Johnston Cobb; p.112 (left) Debra Johnston Cobb, (right) Aba Gyepi-Garbrah; p.114 Aba Gyepi-Garbrah; p.115 Debra Johnston Cobb; p.116 (left/right) Debra Johnston Cobb; p.117 (top/bottom) courtesy Lisa Haspel; p.118 (left/right) Peter H. Tooker & Claudia D. Ward; p.119 (left/centre/right) Ryan Scammell; p.120 (left/right) Aba Gyepi-Garbrah; p.121 Aba Gyepi-Garbrah; p.122-123 Aba Gyepi-Garbrah; p.124 Ryan Scammell; p.125 Ryan Scammell; p.126 (left) Ryan Scammell, (right) Aba Gyepi-Garbrah; p.127 (top/bottom) Aba Gyepi-Garbrah; p.128 Aba Gyepi-Garbrah; p.129 (top/bottom) Aba Gyepi-Garbrah; p.130 Aba Gyepi-Garbrah; p.131 Aba Gyepi-Garbrah; p.132 Aba Gyepi-Garbrah.

The Journey

A Memoir

Phil Miller

You may contact the Author at: philair1@discover-net.net

First Printing, November 2009
Printed in the United States of America

ISBN: 978-0-9823873-4-4

Credits:
        Editor: Clare Brown
        Cover Design: Shawn Buchholz
        Associate Producers: Catherine Stuttgen
                              Suzanne Voros
                              Holliday Alger

Printed by: Publisher's ExpressPress
             Ladysmith, WI

CONTENTS

Dedication

I dedicate this book to my two angels in heaven; my wife, Joan Miller and my granddaughter, Alexandra Voros.

And to my angels here on earth, my daughters, Catherine and Suzanne, son-in-law, John, and grandchildren Caitlin, Cortni, Hannah and Neil.

Chapter One
Introduction

This is one man's life story: me, Phil Miller. This could be the story of a lot of men from anywhere in the world, but it's not. It's the chronicle of a now seventy-four year old man who has lived his dream, and, in the twilight of his life, understands the importance of providing this for his children, grandchildren, other family members, friends and for anyone who has been touched by his life. In a way, this is a snapshot of my life as God's co-pilot.

Sometimes names and dates will be missing because of fading memory, and sometimes out of charity toward those who have been unkind. I will try to recall as best as I can.

A great way to look at life:
1. Free your heart from hatred,
2. Free your mind from worries,
3. Live simply,
4. Give more,
5. Expect Less.

I've learned to surrender to life.

I have a strong faith. You ask what faith means to me? It is believing without seeing, sensing, touching, and hearing. It is a power that circumvents all other power. Prayer was a big part of my survival. It was my wife and her mother who taught me the most about the power of prayer.

Then the question is, "Why not give up?" Well, I think that being a pilot has trained me for living this life that I've been dealt. I have refused to give up, and that is *attitude*. I also plan to have fun every day of my life, for the most part. Fun is planned into my day in my daily calendar.

Pilots are a different kind of people. We have an inborn faith. A unique kind of faith kicks in when you are flying, because it is not normal to fly. Flying gives freedom. It allows for a different perspective on life's problems. You literally step into the hands of God. The pilot's creed is "Take offs are optional, but if you do, you are going to land."

My opinion is that most aircraft accidents are due to pilot error. There is so much in the pilot's hands, from the pre-flight checklist to the pre-departure checklist. And every time I fly, I read these checklists. I get in a zone that says, "I really need to do it right. I don't want to bump into something or the ground." I need to make all of the pre-checks because I can't check something after the fact.

You have to really want to be a pilot. There is not a lot of room to make mistakes or to do wrong things. One of the biggest fears a pilot lives with is not passing their medical exam. A pilot can fly as long as they wish if there are no health issues. But, to hear the words "You can't fly anymore," is gut wrenching.

I don't sleep much – about four or five hours a night. I have been on this earth for over seventy four years, and I don't want to waste my life sleeping.

I have strong self-confidence. It comes from being an avid reader. I take risks, but they are calculated risks. I learned much of what I know on the streets. And I never shirked responsibility.

I love going to church. The reason is because it is a sacred place where I can pause for a moment and think about life. It is the sacredness of the surroundings, the holy place, that allows this. The other benefit of belonging to a church is that it fulfills the need to belong, to be a member of something. It is important to stay grounded by that.

I've had a gifted life. I have lived my dream of airplanes, freedom, airports, family and love. I am at the point in my life where I ask, "Who can I help to live their dream?" I want to and have given back to the world that has given me so much. It is absolutely fun to see others enjoy themselves. It is one thing to read about in a book, but quite another to actually watch someone live their dream and to know that I did something to help them along.

My way of being grateful is not necessarily by praying every day. It is in the act of doing what I love and what I do best. That is how I pray. My doing is my appreciation and thanking my higher power. How one lives their life is their way of giving thanks to God.

I am a person who does answer the phone when it rings. Because I believe that if someone wants you, you are obligated to answer him or her. I take each moment as it comes. You teach others how to treat you. You teach them how to get to you.

Follow-through and following the rules was a big lesson in my life. I have followed the rules, for the most part.

My take in life is different, I bring people together who otherwise wouldn't meet each other. I like that about me.

Chapter Two
Hannah and Her Dolly

On January twenty fifth, two thousand and seven, a beautiful winter day, we boarded an aircraft in Minneapolis. My daughter, Suzanne, her husband, John, and my grandchildren, Hannah and Neil and I were on our way to Big Mountain in Whitefish, Montana, for a skiing vacation. We had taken trips like this many times before, but this time it was different, very different.

I sat away from my family in seat 21A. It was a window seat towards the rear of the aircraft. A young, clean-cut gentleman sat in seat 21C on the aisle. After we reached cruising altitude, my granddaughter Hannah came to sit in 21B right next to me. The young man who was in 21C vacated his seat by moving across the aisle, making the comment, "Looks to me that you two want to talk."

Hannah took my hand and held it for the next two hours, the duration of the flight. During those two hours, Hannah did most of the talking – small talk only a little girl can do. I guess the softness of her hand was what reminded me of her sister, Alexandra, who died at birth. I never met her before that day, but with God's grace through Hannah, I learned all about Alexandra: her soft smile, her gentle touch, her tears, her loving heart, her pure spirit and soft voice were saying, "Hi Grandpa, it's me, Alexandra. Don't cry. I love you, Grandpa." Hold the hand of your third-grade granddaughter if you really want to know what life is all about.

After we landed in Great Falls, Montana, we were informed that the fog had rolled in and our final destination that day, Kalispell, Montana, was closed to air-traffic. We were not allowed to fly, but could take a three to four hour bus ride. Even that ride turned out to be another joy, as it brought us on a tour through Glacier National Park. With towering mountains, the turquoise color of the Flathead River flowing along the side of the road for more than fifty miles, and the elk grazing on the mountainside, it all reminded me of the beauty of the country we live in. Do not close your eyes in this life, or you'll miss what is really important.

Tired from our early start that day, we went to bed early. Hannah came to me and said, "Let's talk. Hazel (her doll) and I will sleep with you tonight as I don't want you to be lonely or sad."

Hannah and her dolly, Hazel

When we woke-up early morning, about four o'clock, my normal wake-up time, Hannah, Hazel and I had a long conversation about the world we live in. I learned that even the bad things that happen are instantly fixed by a nine year old girl and her dolly. They fell back asleep, and I sat there in awe, just soaking up these lessons of life.

It was only nineteen days prior to that that my story was totally different. January sixth, two thousand and seven will forever be etched in my memory. I sat in my easy chair in my home, the

"Salty Dog" watching the NFL playoff games late in the afternoon. I got up to get a drink of water and my legs became weak. I couldn't get to the sink. I sat back down in my chair, feeling a bit dizzy.

I called my sister-in-law Janet and asked her to come over, as my blood pressure cuff was upstairs. She came over to my house right away with her husband Brian. Upon taking my vitals, they found my blood pressure to be 85/45 and I had a heart rate of 32. I knew something was really wrong. From then on, things happened very fast, and they are a little hazy to me.

Janet and Brian took me to the hospital in Stanley, Wisconsin which was only three miles away. I recall as we entered the hospital driveway that the Flight-for-Life helicopter was running on the landing pad. I was surprised, was this helicopter waiting for me, no, it was not for me, there was another patient in the emergency room that had "coded" and they were ready to transfer him to a bigger hospital in Marshfield, Wisconsin. My helicopter ride was to come later.

As many nurses and doctors hovered over me and did their jobs, Father Keith Apfelbeck was there to give me my last rites, again. That's three times he and I have gone through this ritual. I have been at death's door twice before this event. I recall saying to Father, "Do we have to go through this again? Won't I get to heaven this time without the last rites?"

He said, "We will see."

My kidneys had failed. My heart rate was in the twenties, so things looked really bad. I learned later that I was very near death.

As I rode in the helicopter towards Marshfield, the nurse sitting next to me had that look of fear in his eyes. He was scared. The monitor was propped right in front of me, and I could see that things were going downhill pretty fast.

My last memory, as I was being wheeled into the critical care unit at St. Joseph's Hospital in Marshfield, Wisconsin, was of my daughter, Catherine, standing in the hall. I lost all recall for the next twenty two or twenty four hours. I found out later that things had been bad for me throughout the night and the next day. My grandchildren, Caitlin and Cortni their mother Catherine, my sisters-in-law, Joyce, Janet and Mary Jane and brothers-in-law, Brain and Vern did not leave my side the entire time. My granddaughter Caitlin brought me flowers.

LOVE IS OUR HUMAN ROSE
by James Dillet Freeman

"Many flowers grow in many

gardens, but none more beautiful than roses. And in our soul-soil, flowers grow too, but none more beautiful than love— love is our human rose. When I have love in me, I am a garden of roses, and when I am loved, it is as if I have been given a rose bouquet. With love, even a weed-patch life becomes a fragrant garden. O God of love, let this rose, love, bloom in me now,"
(This was found on a card in our family Bible)

Heroic efforts by the medical team aside, I knew that God stepped in and held my hand and said, "My Phil, I'm not ready for you yet." I walked out of that hospital four days later with a skip in my step and a smile on my face. Mismanagement of my medications turned out to be the cause of that episode.

As I have in the past, I wondered what's next? When will the other shoe drop? Am I now going to grow old gracefully? The answers to these questions are made clear day by day.

Chapter Three
From the Beginning…

Merrill and Dorothy Miller

Iwas born on January, twenty first, nineteen thirty five in Augusta, Wisconsin. My mother, Dorothy Miller, told me it was twenty-eight below zero that day. My father, Merrill Miller, had to walk three blocks to get the doctor to come to our house for the birth of yours truly, my parent's third boy. My brother, Charles, was one year older, and he now lives in Sussex, Wisconsin. My oldest brother, Dean, is two years older and now lives in Elkhorn, Wisconsin.

During my adolescence, my father was a civilian test pilot for the U.S. Army Air Corp. We moved around a lot at that time. We lived in several different places, including Colfax, Wausau, and Augusta, Wisconsin; St. Paul, Minnesota; and Billings, Montana.

When my father reached the age of forty, the Army dropped him from the flying program. So, he went to work as a test pilot for what is now known as Northwest Airlines.

At around the time of my fourth or fifth year in school, we moved back to Augusta, Wisconsin. My father became a salesman for M & L Motors in Eau Claire. Wisconsin. During that time, my mother worked at a canning factory in Augusta, Wisconsin That was during World War II, and everyone had a rough time putting food on the table and holding a family together. During wartime, it was hard to make ends meet.

When the war ended, my father bought his first brand-new airplane. It was a 1946, J-3 Cub. It came straight from the factory in Lock Haven, Pennsylvania. He paid seven hundred thirty eight dollars for it and flew it home, landing in a field in Augusta, Wisconsin. As a side-note, I bought my 1946 J-3 Cub, (same as my Dad's) in 2005. It was used and had about 3000 hours on it. I paid thirty six thousand dollars for the same aircraft my father bought for seven hundred thirty eight dollars. Wow! How times have changed.

I went flying with my Dad every chance I could. It was at least once a week for years. He's the one who really taught me about being a pilot. Over the years, he had lots of different airplanes. (Does that sound familiar?) This man could fly anything.

My Dad taught me about life. He taught me to be honest, fight fair, stand up for what you believe, and help someone in need (you don't get paid for everything you do). He taught me to work with commitment, do some community service and also, he taught me that there is punishment for wrongdoing. I have a few marks on my butt from his leather belt to remind me of that.

My mother, Dorothy Harden Miller, taught me about God. She taught me about passion. Whatever you do in life, do the best you can do. She taught me about fair-dealing, kindness to strangers, dancing, singing, working like you don't need the money, smiling, laughing, good hygiene, and building friendships that last a lifetime. For years, my mother was a very committed employee at the Blue Cross Blue Shield Company in Milwaukee, Wisconsin.

When my Dad took off that leather belt of his, I felt a sting. It was my mother's gentle hugs and kisses that were the soothing of my soul. Even though I did some wrong things, I always respected my mother and father. I often think of what my mother and father would have thought of me if they could have watched me journey through this life of mine.

In nineteen fifty two, my father took a sales job at the Alemite Company in Milwaukee, where my family had moved. Because I was a junior in high school, I was allowed to stay in Augusta, Wisconsin to finish high school. In order to stay, I moved in with my Grandma Harden. She owned and operated the Park Hotel and ran it by herself

Park Hotel in Augusta, WI

for fifty-one years. My Grandpa Harden died in nineteen thirty four, a year before I was born.

At the hotel, Grandma had a lot of regular customers. They were mostly salesmen who came into town on the train and stayed a week or so at the hotel. They would set up their products in the hotel garage and usually had big crowds come to see and purchase products from them.

I got to know some of the salesmen. In the evenings, we would all sit and talk for hours in the hotel living room. I think I even got some yearning to be a salesman, just like my dad, from visiting with them.

Although I didn't have to pay my Grandma to live at the hotel, I did have to earn my keep. In the winter, I had to fill the stoker with coal, and in the summer time, mow the massive lawn around the hotel. At least I had my own room and meals made with my grandma's love.

Grandma Harden was a very large woman with a smile that was infectious. She was always happy and had no problem that was so big that she couldn't fix. I do remember many nights when I would come home late from drinking beer (which I was not quite old enough to do) at the Buckhorn Tavern. It is five miles north of Augusta, Wisconsin on Highway 27. It's still there today, in that same location.

Back then, you had to be eighteen years old to drink. At sixteen or seventeen, most of us guys were on the Augusta High Beavers football team. We would catch a ride out to the Buckhorn. More than once, Pinkie, the local cop, would catch us at the Buckhorn, give us hell and then give us a ride back to town.

And every night that I would try to sneak into the hotel at a late hour, Grandma would say, "Phillip, is that you?"

I would answer, "Yes, Grandma."

And she would say, "Have you been drinking beer?"

And I would say, "Yes, Grandma."

She always had the last word. "Phillip, you know you're not old enough to be in a saloon." But by that time, I was half way up the stairs to my room.

I don't remember a lot about my grade school days, but in my days at Augusta High School, my memory serves me better. I was in track, basketball and football. I was number twenty six in basketball and number twenty seven in football. I liked to play ice hockey, but we did not have a team at the school. So on Saturdays and Sundays, after church, we would go downtown and play hockey on the Old Mill Pond. Lots of scars later, I got really good and was asked to play on the men's city team, which was quite an honor.

All through grade school, I had almost perfect attendance. But my senior year in high school was quite different. The fish were biting. What's a boy to do? I chose to go fishing. I'm not sure how I graduated with my class, but I did, in May of nineteen fifty three.

John and Edith Miller

My Grandpa John Miller and Grandma Edith Miller also lived in Augusta. Grandpa John was the owner and operator of a business that provided roller-skating entertainment throughout the area. He would load his trailer with skates, music systems, and concessions and four or five times a week would travel to the surrounding towns and set up his business in their auditoriums or other available facilities. He rented out roller-skates to people who came to skate and provided

music and snacks, chips and things like that. It
seemed like everyone had a great time.

Grandpa made a nice living at that business.
I went to help him out many times. Grandma
Edith was always by his side, helping with the
business too. Looking back now, I think I learned
some of my entrepreneurial skills from Grandpa
Miller.

I was very young when he died. I was with
him at his desk, and he was getting his last night
receipts ready to take to the bank, when he just fell
over dead, right in front of me. This was the first
time in my life that I was in the presence of death.
Little did I understand about death being a part of
life. This would not be the last time I experienced
being in death's presence.

My Grandma Edith lived for a very long
time after Grandpa Miller died. I remember her
being the best cook on the planet. I went to see her
all of the time, and she always had some fresh
baked things for me. Spending time with
grandparents is definitely the definition of love.

Several years later, my high school friend,
Marvin, and I were riding our Cushman motor
scooters back from Osseo, Wisconsin where we
both had girlfriends. When we got to Augusta, at
the intersection of Highways 12 and 27, Marvin's
scooter hit a patch of ice and slid under a bulk gas
truck that was passing in front of us. His life was

snuffed out from him in an instant. Losing a friend is one of the most painful parts of life. Earning friends is the joy of life, but it is hard for your brain to process the loss of one of these friends. So, always keep them in your heart.

During my high school years, I always had a job. During the day, I worked on the threshing crews, and at night I worked at the canning factory. I remember that my first canning factory job paid forty two cents an hour, and was I ever thrilled.

Since I had gotten my driver's license, I really wanted my own car. I finally got it. It was a 1924 model T, four-door, which I bought for twenty dollars from a fellow named Guy Terry. He was the caretaker at the Lake Eau Claire Pavilion. I owned that car throughout the rest of my high school days.

My English teacher, Miss Zank, married a gentleman named Mr. Morgan, and I got a part-time job at their dry cleaning business. Years later, Mrs. Morgan moved to Thorp, Wisconsin and taught high school English. As a matter of fact, she taught both of my daughters, Catherine and Suzanne. A few years ago, I built a duplex in Thorp and guess who lived in one of them? You guessed it: Mrs. Morgan.

Another event I remember from growing up happened while we were living in St. Paul,

Minnesota. There was a kid who shot an arrow at me. I told my brothers about it, but I didn't tell my mom right away.

My brothers and I built a set of stocks – you know, the kind you put your head and hands in. We caught the kid at the start of the school day and put him in there and locked it. We went to school and left him in there. He was in there the entire day. Talk about capital punishment!

To top that off, I told my mother about the arrow incident, and she went over to his home and beat him up, black eyes and all. The moral of the story: do not mess with my mother or me.

We listened to the radio a lot. There were no televisions then, so for our news, we listened to the radio or we would go to the theater on Friday nights, as they would have fifteen-minute news specials about the war just before the movie. I remember listening to the radio on December seventh, nineteen forty one, when they announced the beginning of our participation in World War II. It was the day of the bombing of Pearl Harbor.

Back then we had ration stamps for sugar, coffee, butter, and other food items. My dad also had ration stamps for gasoline, tires, batteries, and the other items for his automobile. It was the only way a person could buy those items, and a lot of times, one could trade stamps with someone else for money to make other purchases.

It was after a high school basketball game that my friend Wayne Shong gave me a ride home. I told him that our driveway was a slippery slope and that he should go slowly. Well, he didn't and guess what? We crashed right through the garage door. That's another time I felt the sting of my father's leather belt.

As a kid, we played *Kick the Can* and *Annie, Annie Over* and *Hide N' Seek*. We tipped over lots of out-houses, cooned some watermelons, and dipped the girl's braids in the inkwells on our desk at school. Those were some of the mischievous things I recall in my early years.

I do remember that one Halloween a group of us took the big merry-go-round apart and, like fools, we carried it up the outside fire-escape to the school house roof; and put it all back together. All this time, Pinky, the local cop, was watching us. When we finished putting it all together, he put the red lights on and shone the spotlight right on us. He got out his bullhorn and told us to take it all apart and bring it back down and put it back together where it belonged. We worked all night and I think until about noon the next day to get it all done. So our prank backfired on us and, needless to say, another whipping from the leather belt was in store for me.

The time we hitchhiked to see the Minnesota State Fair is very clear to me still. It seems as though we wanted to go pretty badly, but didn't dare tell our folks. So a couple of friends and I hitchhiked there. We didn't have any trouble getting a ride there. We stayed all day until dark. However, we soon discovered that it wasn't going to be so easy getting back. Since I was the ringleader, I had to call my father to come and get us. I had to call collect too. Needless to say, when we got home, it was leather-belt time.

But some of our pranks were successful. I remember the time we caught a freight train to Wausau. It was a new train, and we rode in a boxcar just for the fun of it. Luckily, we jumped another freight train in Wausau and returned home, and no one ever knew about it.

Chapter Four
Becoming a Man

It was May nineteenth, nineteen fifty three when I graduated from high school. I wanted to go on to college, but we didn't have the money, so I moved to Milwaukee and got a job. I moved in with a bunch of friends. Elmer Zillmer helped me get a job at Briggs & Stratton, a manufacturer of engines. I remember they started me out at one dollar and three cents per hour, plus piecework. I thought that I had reached the big time. I wasn't there for long, though. My Grandma Harden called and said, "Phillip, you need to come as soon as possible. You just received a letter from the President of the United States."

The Korean War – wait, we didn't call it that then. The draft for the Korean Police Action was

on. When I opened the letter, it said that I was to
report to the United States Army at the St. Paul,
Minnesota induction center on October eighth,
nineteen fifty three. Yes, I was drafted into the
military.

Phil in the Army

There are times in your life when everything
just goes numb. This was one of those times.
"What the hell," I said to myself. "I was only
eighteen years old, how could they do this to me?"

On that October day, I boarded an Army
train in St. Paul for our trip to the basic training
base at Fort Riley, Kansas. This was my

introduction into manhood. Upon arrival at Fort Riley, our heads were shaved, and we stood in line for a lot of shots. And then it was off to the supply room where received one set of a GI uniform.

The First Sergeant told us to remove every bit of our civilian clothing, put it in a box and send it to our mothers. That's when the reality of it all hit, and it really got to me. I cried the entire night.

The next sixteen weeks were spent in basic training. We were instructed about how to use our weapons, an M-16 rifle and all the other gear. They worked us hard all week, but we had Saturday and Sunday off.

During basic training, we did not get off-base passes. The ritual was that on Friday nights, we would go down by the fence to watch all the GI's that did have passes hook up with a lineup of girls from Kansas State University. After several trips to the fence and seeing all of those girls, some with lots of cleavage, I went to my First Sergeant and asked if I could go to the dispensary. When he asked me why I wanted to go, I told him that I was not getting an erection, so there must be something wrong with me. He laughed, and explained that there was nothing wrong with me as all new recruits in basic training were fed saltpeter, and after basic training was over, all of my bodily functions would return to normal. Those bastards.

They worked us until we dropped. They

made us get up and work in the early morning. More than once, I was ready to throw in the towel, but I couldn't. I remembered what my dad taught me, which was to never give up. Before we could enter the mess hall, we would have to do chin-ups in the doorway. If we didn't do enough chin-ups, we didn't get to eat. There were a lot of guys who couldn't do them, including me. So more often than not, we went to the PX and got a snack – that is, if we had the money.

When I got my first pay, I earned seventy two dollars per month. We got it in cash. I sent fifty dollars home for my car payment. With the twenty-two dollars in cash I had left over, I would look for the guys who were playing cards and shooting dice. I would lend them a ten-dollar bill with their promise to pay me back twenty dollars earned from gambling. I usually sat and watched and collected money and interest before moving on to another game. Whenever I got to have one hundred dollars in my hand, which was most of the time, I left. This is where I learned a bit about financial transactions.

After sixteen weeks of basic training, I looked at the reassignment board every day for over two weeks before I saw my posting. It read as follows: Miller, Philip N., Private, US 55410302 is assigned to sixteen weeks of advanced basic training. There was no location and the start date listed for that next training was put on hold. Those bastards.

Finally, it was off to Charleston, South Carolina. It was an Army Medical Aide and Training School. Eventually I was assigned to an Army Ranger Company at Camp Rucker in Alabama. Now these guys are really crazy bastards. With them, it was off to a Navy ship off the coast of Florida. They dumped us in the ocean, with just our clothing and life vests, and the ship sailed away. There we were, a bunch of kids, bobbing around in the ocean filled with who the hell knows what. Sharks, we feared. We held ourselves together in a big circle during the night and nearly froze our asses off. Late the next day, after being burnt to a crisp in the hot sun, the ship picked us up. All of us looked like salt-water pickles.

After that, we were off to live for three or four weeks with the crazies in the swamps of the Florida Everglades. We built living quarters in the trees and slept in hammocks built from Cyprus tree vines. We ate whatever we could find, gator or plants – whatever the crazies, um, I mean the Army Rangers, could find. These guys were really nuts.

Then guess what? They shipped us off to the snowy mountains in the state of Washington. And with the crazies, we pitched our tent in the snowfields, where we lived again for three or four weeks. We were trained to ski, and we had special assault training. This is where I learned to use a 45-caliber grease gun. During this ranger training phase, I saw a number of guys die of coral snake bites, water moccasin bites, and Black Widow spider bites, or even freeze to death after being lost in the blinding snow. But Army soldiers are expendable: the Army would just draft some more to fill the spots of those they lost.

Finally, I got to leave the crazies and return to an assignment at an Army medical center unit hospital at Camp Rucker, Alabama. Finally, it was back to civilization. It wasn't long before the Army decided to convert Camp Rucker, Alabama to Fort Rucker and make it a helicopter-training base. So our division, the 29th division, was reassigned to Fort Benning, Georgia. Of course, our smart-ass General decided that it would be good training to walk. We marched the entire hundred miles or so from Fort Rucker to Fort Benning.

At Fort Benning, I was assigned to the officer's training school parachute training unit and the base morgue. At the drop zone, I saw a lot of guy's chutes malfunction and drop to their death. It was my job to pick up their bodies and take them to the morgue.

It was at Fort Benning that I was promoted to Sergeant. My pay increased to one hundred forty four dollars per month and remained that until my final discharge from the Army. At Fort Benning, most of my weekends were free. I would go into town: Columbus, Georgia. It was a USO town, where there were lots of nice girls to dance and drink beer with and things like that. I didn't have a girlfriend at home, so it was a nice place to meet some girls.

At Christmastime, the USO asked the GIs to come and each would be invited into someone's home for Christmas. Since I didn't have a leave during that time, I went to the USO and one of the girls invited me to her parents' home for Christmas dinner. I had danced with her before, and she was a very nice person. So, she picked me up with her car and took me to her parents' home. I remember driving up this long driveway. It was a mansion with butlers and servants all over the place. I was stunned, as I never imagined this young lady's parents to be very, very rich.

As I entered their home, I was very scared. But in an instant I saw that these people were very, very nice and down to earth. They were so very thankful for having a GI in their home, as they had no sons, and they treated me with respect and kindness. We had a great time. Over the next several months, I was back there many times, and they became true friends.

Being a medical aid required me to work at

times in the base dispensary. There were many times when the MPs would come in for a penicillin shot because they caught some blue balls or something else from some girl over in Phoenix City, Alabama. Well, I wasn't about to let a golden opportunity go by. In exchange for giving one MP his shot, I asked him to find me an Army Colt 45-pistol with a pearl handle and metal chrome work. Lo and behold, he brought two of them to me.

The day of my discharge finally arrived on October seventh, nineteen fifty five. My car was on the base, so I loaded it full of stuff. I promised to take two buddies back to their homes, one in Boston and the other in Cleveland.

The Army tried to get us to re-enlist that day, but knowing we were free, I chose my discharge. With my discharge bonus of eighteen hundred dollars in hand, we headed for the main gate.

The MPs checked our paperwork and looked through my car. They found the pistols under my front seat, and when they asked, I told them I didn't know how they got there. Not wanting to stay and explain, I let them take the pistols, and we were gone.

After two weeks and a lot of fun, I arrived home in Milwaukee. I had less than one hundred dollars in my pocket when I got there, so it must have been a lot of fun.

Chapter Five
You Are So Beautiful to Me

Finally, my dream was going to come true. I was to receive three hundred twenty eight dollars per month to go to college from the G.I. Bill. With that and a part-time job at Norm's Texaco station, I could pursue a degree. I moved in with my parents in Milwaukee and enrolled at Milwaukee State Teachers College, which is now the University of Wisconsin, Milwaukee. Even though the fall semester had begun, as a veteran, I was allowed to start late.

Just after the first of the year, my friends in Augusta wanted me to come to see them again, as it had been more than two years since I'd visited them. It was January twenty first nineteen fifty six, my twenty-first birthday. A few of us decided to go out that night to drink some beer and do some dancing. We chose an old beer joint and dance hall called the *Hoot* in Hallie, Wisconsin, near Eau Claire.

Joan Hedler, My Future Wife

I remember I was standing there with a beer in my hand when I saw her. She was walking directly toward me. I tried to look away, but I thought, "Wow, you are so beautiful." I was wearing an Army t-shirt that said *U.S. Army Korean Veteran*. She said, "Excuse me, are you in the Army?"

I said, "Not any more. I was discharged on October seventh."

She asked me why I had come to the *Hoot* that night, and I told her that I was celebrating my twenty-first birthday. I said, "I like to drink beer and dance with my friends and chose to come to the *Hoot,* and here we are."

She said, "Well, then let's dance."

I think we danced together every dance after that until closing time. I asked her name, and she said, "Joan."

After closing, she said, "How about a cup of coffee?"

I said, "Sure."

That was fifty-three years ago.

She suggested the Litchfield Cafe in Eau Claire on Highway 12, as it was open all night. There we drank coffee and smoked cigarettes and talked until dawn. We learned a lot about each other. We fell in love immediately, and it lasted almost fifty years.

I learned that her name was Joan Catherine Hedler. She was from Thorp, Wisconsin. She was currently living in St. Paul, Minnesota and attending airline stewardess school, the McConnell. She preferred to be called "Joann" even though her name was spelled J-O-A-N. She was going to stay with her mother and father in

Thorp, Wisconsin that night, and before I could get her phone number, she had driven away.

Her sister told her that I stayed with my Grandma Harden at the Park Hotel in Augusta whenever I was up north, so she knew how to get a-hold of me. But I had no idea how to get a-hold of her.

Sure enough, sometime early the following week, my grandma told me that someone called and left a phone number where I could reach them. When I called the number, Joan answered, and asked me to meet her the following Saturday afternoon at the Litchfield Caf . She got a ride from St. Paul and wanted me to take her to Thorp to meet her family. There was a blizzard that Friday, and there was snow everywhere. I left Milwaukee early Saturday morning, but the drive took forever. Some hours later, there she was, waiting for me. We sat and talked for a while and then realized it was after ten at night, so we started for Thorp.

I remember arriving at her parent's house at 12:45 a.m. When we drove into the Hedler yard, the house was dark. It was the first time she gave me a real hug and kiss. She got out and watched as I tried to move the car a little, but I was stuck in the snow. She jumped back into the car and said, "Don't worry; I'll give you a push with my Dad's beer truck."

Well, instead of just pulling up behind me and giving me a gentle nudge, she had to be going probably ten or fifteen miles an hour when she gave me that push, and when I looked back, I saw her mother on the porch. I got so scared that I just kept on going and headed for Augusta. What a great impression I must have made! The following weekend I met her family: her mother, Mary, and her father, Leo; her brother, Jerome; and her four sisters, Jackie, Janet, Mary Jane, and Joyce.

In the spring, we picked out a ring together, a ring for which she had to pay. We were engaged to be married. She quit airline school and moved to Milwaukee. She got an apartment and a job working for Milwaukee County. I continued to attend college. We planned our wedding and got married September eighth, nineteen fifty six at St. Bernard's Church in Thorp, Wisconsin. I still belong to that parish to this day. I converted from Lutheranism to her Roman Catholic faith. It was then that I really started my journey to know about faith.

It was a real Polish wedding, lasting three days. We got ready on Friday, had the wedding on Saturday, and on Sunday, we opened presents. It was so much fun, and it will be etched in my mind forever. On Monday, we left for our honeymoon. It was a little cabin on Chetek Lake in northern Wisconsin. We fished all day and at night, we got

Joan and Phil after the Wedding

to know one another. And of course, something funny had to happen. Because it was fall, the temperatures cooled down in the evening. In the cabin, we had a little wood-burning stove that kept the chill out. Well you might've guessed it: on the way to the bathroom in the middle of the night, I burned my Johnson on that wood-burning stove. For the rest of our honeymoon, all we did was fish, and of course, she caught all the fish.

That was the start of a very happy, loving, and fun life together for the next almost forty-eight years.

"Love is patient, love is kind. It does not envy, it does not boast, it is not proud. It is not rude, it is not self-

*seeking, it is not easily angered, it keeps
no record of wrongs. Love does not
delight in evil but rejoices with the truth.
Love bears all things, believes all things,
hopes all things, endures all things. Love
never ends." —(1 Corinthians 13: 4-8)*

You are so beautiful to me.

We rented our first apartment, near Milwaukee, in Wauwatosa, Wisconsin. Joan went back to work, and I went back to college. I think we paid sixty dollars per month for that apartment. I do know that it was hard to pay rent and buy food. So lots of times, we would show-up at my parent's home just before supper and, of course, we ate supper with them. The kitchen in that apartment was so small only one person at a time could be in there. In the bedroom, there was just enough room for a mattress on the floor. No dressers or anything. We had to go in and out through the doorway one at a time. In the living room, where we ate, you could sit on the couch, and if you put your feet up, you could touch the other wall. I stayed in school for another year or so, but wanted to help out with the bills, so I dropped out of school. My wife didn't like that, but I needed to be the bread winner in our marriage.

My wife and I were together for forty-eight years. During that time, there were so many things that made our life special. We seemed to celebrate every holiday – the birthdays of the kids, and any other reason to celebrate we could find. She always knew how to throw a party. She would bring out the Spoed china, our best, for Thanksgiving and Christmas and other holidays too.

I remember there was always too much food. No matter how many people came, there was always too much food. Our house was a gathering place for all of our relatives. Joan and I took care to make sure everyone felt just as important as the next person. At Christmas time, we had to have Santa Claus show up for the kids. He always did too. During the winter, we skied, went snowmobiling and always included the children in everything we did. In the springtime, she would pack the camper full of goodies, and the minute school was out, we would be off to Canada for our annual fishing trip.

Our summer times were filled with graduation parties, weddings, and anniversaries. Joan would not leave the house without looking just so, and Sundays were always real dress-up days for her.

One day I told her that I wanted to take her to Alaska. I remembered she mentioned to me once that I had been there a number of times, but reminded me that she hadn't. So, one Friday afternoon, I came home from a selling trip and asked her to pack her bags. The kids were all off living their lives, so we had nothing holding us back.

She asked me, "Why?"

I said, "Well, because we are going to Alaska." You should have seen the look on her face when I told her we were leaving Monday.

We flew to Seattle and then on to Anchorage and rented a car and drove all over the Kenai Peninsula – to a number of glaciers and to gold mines, where we panned for gold. We fished in the Kenai National Wild Refuge and this little town at the very tip of the peninsula called Homer. And what did we see parked and abandoned on the edge of the beach? A school bus that had *Osseo-Fairchild School District* printed on the side of it. We were so far from home, and here we saw a bus from a town thirty-five miles away from us back in Wisconsin! We stayed in Alaska until we finally

Cessna Cardinal

both got tired. One day we looked at each other and said, "Let's go home." So we called the airlines the next day and went home.

We went on a lot more trips like that. She and I would jump in my Cessna Cardinal and fly from our North Fork airstrip to the Apostle Islands in Lake Superior. We would have lunch and turn around and fly back the same day. It was such fun.

There were many times when I would jump in my plane and fly to La Crosse, Wisconsin to pick up the girls and fly them home from college. It was part of our lifestyle.

Joan was an awesome seamstress and quilter. She made quilts for everyone. She also did a lot of cross-stitch and made a number of pictures. They are a constant reminder of her creativity and many of her works hang in my home today. Joan taught me to dance the polka, and we both loved to go to dances. Every opportunity we could, we would get out and go dancing.

Joan was no homebody. She was always ready to go if we decided to go someplace and take our children. Whether it was jumping in the camper to go fishing, flying to Montana to ski, or heading to Fort Lauderdale, Florida to hit the beach, she was ready to go.

I loved how she always kept me looking good. She praised me for how handsome I was and made sure that I always was dressed properly and neatly for every occasion.

Joan was that way with the whole family. When our oldest was born, Catherine, I remember she had a little piece of skin on one of her ears. Joan was very concerned about this. Before you knew it, they had cut it off and handed us our perfect little girl.

When Suzanne was born, I knew she was ours because I could hear her screaming like crazy. What a beautiful blonde bombshell she was. I call her the "Tiger from Thorp."

Both Catherine and Suzanne are as different as night and day. There are some similarities, though, like their dedication to their respective professions. Catherine, the teacher, and Suzanne, the nurse, are perfect when it comes to grooming, like their mother. And they both have their father's toughness. But the big difference between the two is that Catherine is a non-stop talker. In fact, I think she talks in her sleep. Suzanne is much more reserved. She is forever trying to figure things out for herself.

I remember when Catherine was small. She always got her Dad to take her down to the river to fish. She loved to play with the worms. And to show you how kids copy their parents, there was this time when Suzanne was in the backyard sandbox. When I walked down to see what was going on, I could hear her saying, "Those Goddamned flies." It didn't take her long to learn that from her father!

Their days at the Thorp School were spent with some pretty special friends. I remember so many parties at the dining room table, rides on the snowmobile and 3-wheeler, or just playing in the backyard.

Both of the girls have their father's drive and their mother's kindness. It is fun now that they are grown with families of their own to enjoy some of the same things with them that we did when they were younger. Now, though, we take the grandkids along. My oldest granddaughter, Caitlin, graduated from Assumption High School in two thousand and eight. She is the ultimate lady. She takes after her mother, Catherine. She is the kind of kid you want your children and grandchildren to turn out to be like. She is not only a good student; she is a good friend too.

Cortni, Catherine's youngest daughter, is the girl who tackles anything. She is very competitive in her sports. She loves to fly with me. She is an awesome artist and hopefully will continue to develop that talent. Both girls are talented musicians. They play in the school bands and perform in the musicals, which is great source of entertainment.

My other granddaughter, Suzanne's daughter, Hannah, and her brother, Neil, are dedicated to their swim teams. Hannah likes good music and they are both hard workers. Neil loves football and softball. I think he will follow in Grandpa's footsteps and become a pilot.

Whether we are all together or I take the girls and their families separately, we always have fun. Even before their grandmother passed away, we made annual pilgrimages someplace in the country, together as a family. I think that this is an offshoot from the lives Joan and I led as children. These times together give rise to the small talk that ties our lives together, bonding us together.

A few years ago, we did something really different. We went off to Glacier National Park in Montana for some whitewater rafting: Suzanne, John, Hannah, Neil and Grandpa, barreling down that Flathead River in a rubber raft. What an awesome adventure!

White Water Rafting

Neil at Hungry Horse Dam

We also explored some backcountry and went trout fishing, high up in the mountains on the south end of Hungry Horse Dam.

Chapter Six
A Different Life

As I said previously, I decided to leave college after Joan and I got married, though my young wife wasn't thrilled about the idea. A friend of mine from college told me about a brand-new manufacturing company that was looking for employees, Marquette Cement Company. They were producers of cement powder and were building a new plant on Canal Street in the Menomonee River Valley in Milwaukee.

I applied and got a job operating a D-7 bulldozer, pushing limestone, sand, and coal into various hoppers to feed the plant.

The pay was great: four dollars and one cent per hour. It was a full-time, shift-work job. The work schedule changed every two weeks from days to afternoons to nights. It was my first real job.

About that same time, my wife got a new job working for General Motors in south Milwaukee on the Titan Missile Program. She loved that job. We even moved into a house in Brown Deer, Wisconsin. It was sixteen miles from her work in the city, but she loved it.

I think we rented that house for eighty five dollars a month, but we could afford it, as we had now hit what we thought was the big-time. No more hot dogs and beans. We could now afford to eat meat and potatoes and live what we thought was a normal and prosperous life. After less than a year working at Marquette Cement, I got promoted to the yard foreman and then sometime later to shipping superintendent, which included a raise. I was now making five dollars per hour.

We worked at trying to have children, but nothing seemed to happen. I hoped it wasn't because of the burn on my Johnson at that little honeymoon cabin.

I stayed with Marquette Cement until the spring of nineteen sixty two. Two former executives, Carl Hauser and Sam Webb, who had left Marquette Cement, called me to talk about a new job possibility. They wanted to know if I would consider moving to New York State and work for them at a place that was being built called Atlantic Cement. They were just in the building phase and they wanted me onboard. My wife and I discussed this job in detail. We would have to move away from our current jobs, our families, and our now comfortable living. Together, we said, "Let's go for it;" and we did.

So in nineteen sixty two, we went to upstate New York, near Albany, to look for a place to live. We found a new three-bedroom house on Picard Road in Voorheesville, New York. The builder wanted eleven thousand dollars and I could not afford that, so I finally got him down to nine thousand, one hundred dollars. We bought the house and moved in. What a beautiful location – tucked up against the Helderburg Mountains. It was only about ten or twelve miles to my new job in Ravena, New York, which was along the Hudson River. Joan also got a job working in Albany for the New York State Legislature.

This was my first job as a salaried person. I was the Shipping Superintendent in charge of loading ocean-going barges. The company owned three barges, sixteen thousand tons apiece, that carried cement powder. These barges were about four hundred feet long, sixty feet wide, and thirty feet deep and were pushed by a three thousand five hundred horsepower, tugboat. The barges were named Adelaide, Andrea, and Alexandra. From our facilities on the Hudson River in upstate New York, shipments were made along the entire East coast.

I believe my first salary was seven thousand two hundred dollars a year, which seemed like a lot to me. It wasn't long before I was promoted to Distribution Station Superintendent. I was responsible for managing our entire distribution network. Each of our distribution locations were at seaports, except for one. They were Boston, Massachusetts; Brooklyn, New York; Bayonne, New Jersey; Baltimore, Maryland; Norfolk, Virginia; Savannah, Georgia; Jacksonville, Florida; Cape Canaveral, Florida; Fort Lauderdale, Florida; Tampa, Florida; and Charlotte, North Carolina. I had to set up the distribution locations by hiring people and overseeing the training and operations of the work. I was also put in charge of the marine operations. That meant I had to see that the barges were unloaded at each port and scheduled properly.

The I.L.A. had jurisdiction over all the port operations at every one of these ports. It wasn't long before I was in a taxi on my way to their headquarters, located at 1 Court St. in Brooklyn, New York. When I told my taxi-driver where I wanted him to take me, he said, "Are you going there alone? You must be crazy."

Little did I know.

As I recall, there were no windows on the first four floors of this five-story, brick building. There was just a door that led to an elevator. The elevators had no up and down buttons, but as you entered, the elevator was operated remotely, and it took me up to the fifth floor. When I got off the elevator, I was met by a guy wearing a shoulder holster and firearm. As a matter of fact, there were thugs all over the place wearing shoulder holsters and carrying firearms. Yes, I was crazy. I was escorted to a large office with plush carpet, wood-paneled walls, overstuffed chairs and couches, and a large mahogany desk with not one single piece of paper on it.

I thought to myself, "What the hell is going on here?" I thought we were making a movie or something. I remember thinking I could not let my bosses down; I decided to straighten these guys out.

There I met _____ and his brother-in-law, _____. They were dressed to a tee. They were both in charge of the I.L.A. _____'s father died in a blaze of gunfire, specifically mob gunfire, in a barbershop in Brooklyn several years earlier. They explained to me that every time a barge was to be unloaded at one of the ports, it required the hiring of an unloading gang, which consists of twenty-seven people and a foreman from the I.L.A. union. At that time, the fee for this was about thirty thousand dollars a day.

So, here I was. This kid from Augusta, Wisconsin in New York City was going to show these guys something. I explained to them that our barges were self-unloading and required no employees. We were usually in port for no more than eight hours, where the crew would hook up the hoses to our receivers and the on-board barge pumps would pump the cement powder into the shore storage systems.

They were not impressed. They very bluntly repeated their earlier requirements or suggested that perhaps I could come up with some other accommodation (i.e. payoff). I came up with a plan whereby we would give them ten thousand dollars in cash, which I delivered myself to the man in charge at each port. The options were limited, either to pay the ten thousand dollars or hire the twenty seven people plus a foreman and pay the thirty thousand dollars a day. This was a no brainier to me.

When I made my final deal with _____, I said, "You asked me to come up with some accommodations. Here is mine." I never told him that I wouldn't do what he wanted. I never said no to them. I never refused to hire his twenty seven people; instead, I handed him ten thousand dollars. Because it was cash, we got along just fine, with no problems from that day forward. I thought I was big stuff because I was wearing three hundred fifty dollar suits, cashmere overcoats, and carried a leather briefcase. All my corporate superiors ever said to me that I was doing a great job.

All of a sudden, I was in the underworld. I met with those guys so many times that we actually became friends even though they were criminals. I respected them because their word was their word. I was safe as I traveled the East Coast, and I was safe for two reasons. They had the best communication system, for one. Everyone knew that Phil Miller was the paymaster. And secondly, I upheld my end of the deal. Five days a week for the next five years, they protected me because I constantly carried large sums of money that were used to pay their people at various ports.

Amazingly, we always got unloaded no matter if there was a strike or not. It would go like this. When the barge was in say, Savannah, I would call their office and they would send two guys down to the port for unloading. I gave them cash, including a payoff for their union boss; everybody went away happy, and our barges got unloaded. Once though, there was a strike in Jacksonville, Florida during one of the times we were unloading our barge. A fellow competitive cement company next door to me said, "I'll never pay bribes." He accused me of taking all of his business.

Quite often, after meeting with _____ and _____, we would go to the Waldorf-Astoria for lunch. They had their limousine parked in a no-parking zone. They paid a cop to watch the vehicle while we had lunch. It showed me that everybody they touched was on the take. It's my belief it remains that way to this very day.

I remember one time when I got back to my office there were ten tickets sent to me for a Maritime Port Council Dinner in New York City at the Waldorf. The tickets cost a thousand dollars each. When I talked to my boss, he told me that he wasn't going to pay. So, _____ called him, and he changed his mind.

I went to the Council Dinner by myself. And lo and behold, the head table had quite a mixture of folks, _____, Hollywood stars, the Bishops, the police commissioners, mayors and lots of judges and Chiefs of Police and, of course, a mixture of priests and other dignitaries from the various boroughs of New York City. It was something to see. Ninety percent of them were thugs. As I sat there, I thought, "Holy Shit! What the hell did I get myself into?"

(This part is the only part of my life that I didn't disclose to Joan during our entire marriage. I knew if I told her about it, she would be worried all of the time. I was constantly traveling. So, she never knew about my connections to the underworld. As a matter of fact, no one else knew either.)

All of the guys I was connected to during

that period are now dead or in federal prison, so I feel like I can talk about it. Even my boss had no idea. He just kept supplying me with the cash, and I got the job done. No questions asked.

With all the airline travel that I did during that time, some funny things happened. I usually flew Mohawk Airlines to New York City from Albany and then on down the coast to the various other locations. I remember that one time the plane I was supposed to fly had trouble at the Albany airport. I decided that I would drive to New York City and then fly on from there to Florida and other locations I was visiting. On the way back, one Friday night, I was anxious to get home. I went to the Albany airport parking lot to get my car, but my car wasn't there. So I thought my car had been stolen. I called the police and told them my car was stolen from the parking lot at the Albany airport and took a cab home.

The next day as Joan and I sat and talked, I told her about the stolen car. She told me I should have never driven it to New York City because the odds of getting it stolen were very high there. New York City? Sure enough, I had screwed up. I took a flight to New York City and there sat my car in the parking lot, just where I had left it.

Another crazy thing happened to me as I drove my car to the Boston airport and drove through the tollbooths; I remember I gave the attendant a twenty dollar bill. The attendant told me to please pull over to the side of the road, and when I did, two people came up to my car door in an instant. They showed me their badges and put me in handcuffs and took me downtown to the Treasury Department. It appeared that I had paid the toll with a counterfeit twenty dollar bill. They then asked me to go through my wallet and produce all of the twenty dollar bills I had. Well, wouldn't you know, I had just cashed an expense check and, of course, I had plenty of twenty dollar bills. I believe it was over one hundred dollars. Together, we called my boss and confirmed my identity and so forth, and they finally said they'd take me back to my auto. When I asked for a receipt for the money they kept, they said it wasn't money, it was counterfeit. So, I was out the money.

Another time my boss called and said, "Phil, one of our barges got caught in a hurricane near Jacksonville, Florida. It had broken loose from the tug and was floating out to sea. The tug then abandoned the barge and returned to port. I rented a plane, and for over two weeks, I flew in four-hour shifts up and down the coast of the Atlantic. I would land to get fuel and go to the bathroom, and then fly another four hours. Every day I was scanning the Atlantic Ocean for the barge. Do you know how big the Atlantic Ocean is?

Finally, the Coast Guard called and advised

us that they had found our barge; it was about forty miles off the coast of Puerto Rico, near San Juan. They agreed to fly me to the barge and drop me on the deck of the barge, so I could get the engines started to allow a tug to hook to it. Well, about the time that I got to the deck of the barge, a sea swell raised the barge. When they dropped me, they slammed me into the deck, released me from the helicopter harness, and said good-bye.

I called my office and asked them what they wanted me to do with this barge full of cement. They advised me to try and sell it to the Ponce Puerto Rico Cement Company. I did that at a discount. With the tug pushing the barge, we sailed to the south side of the island. When we got within the port area, the Ponce civil administration insisted that a harbor master take charge of the vessel as it came into port. With that, the harbor master climbed onboard and took over guiding the barge towards the unloading dock. I told him that he needed to go very slow as this barge had sixteen thousand tons of cement on it and only a bow thruster. In no uncertain terms, he told me he was in charge and knew what he was doing and didn't like my idea of telling him what to do. Needless to say, as we approached the eight hundred foot long dock, he couldn't slow the barge down. He wiped the dock off the face of the earth and beached the barge. So for several days, a bunch of people floated the hoses on oil barrels out to the barge, and we finally got it off the beach. The dock looked like a bunch of toothpicks floating in the bay.

At last, the job was done. At the Ponce airport, I saw two guys in white bib overalls with grease all over them get into this airplane. So I boarded a Ponce Airways, oil-leaking DC-7. What a bunch of junk. We flew at treetop level back to San Juan. I was not just a passenger, but THE passenger. It appeared that they had just fixed the plane. In San Juan, I boarded an American aircraft back to New York. You've got to be crazy to fly Ponce Airways.

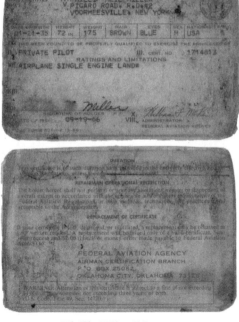

Phil's Pilot License

It was while we lived in New York that I finally took flying lessons and got my private pilot licenses. It had been a dream since my early childhood and, finally, that dream came true. It cost me three hundred dollars for the entire program. The airstrip was only two miles from my home and Dan, the owner and flight instructor, was a wonderful person. He taught me in an Aeronca Champ. I took my flight tests in a Piper Tri-Pacer. Finally, I was living my dream. Finally, I was a private pilot, just like my dad.

One day, my wife said to me, "Honey, I'm pregnant." After eleven years of marriage, we finally had the start of our family. Catherine Mary was born in Albany Medical Center on May thirtieth nineteen sixty seven. What a bundle of joy! Now I knew what life was all about. The day of her birth, I went flying.

You are so beautiful to me.

With a baby daughter to raise, I needed to get away from the daily traveling and, even more so, from the underworld connection. At that time, there was only one thug left who knew my identity. Then, a police friend of mine in Bayonne, New Jersey called me and told me that this person had died in an auto accident. I was now free. I could now leave, and I did.

In early nineteen sixty eight, I got a new job. One of my former bosses called me and said he was affiliated with Martin Marietta Corporation, a huge multinational company, and he wanted me to take over the operations of a cement plant in Martinsburg, West Virginia. I took the job at once. We moved into an old company house on the property that didn't even have a stove, so we cooked on a hotplate. I remember that the baby crib for Catherine would roll to one side of the room because the floors were crooked. It was makeshift, but I was happy to be there.

I remember meeting a building contractor named Rodney Chessman. He built a new house for us on North Red Hill Road in Martinsburg, West Virginia. He wanted twenty one thousand dollars for this home, which I thought I could not afford. But the banker in town extended me a loan because I was a big shot at the Capitol Cement Company.

During my days at Martin Marietta Corporation, I used to call for the corporate jet and would take a lot of our customers down to the Masters Golf Tournament in Augusta, Georgia. Those were the days Arnold Palmer, Gary Player, Tom Wisecoff, and Jack Nicholas played. It was an era of great golf and watching these pros play golf was a lot of fun. It was an annual thing we did for our customers.

Then on February first nineteen sixty nine, our family grew again with the birth of Suzanne

Marie. My Tiger from Thorp was born at King's Daughter Hospital in Martinsburg, WV. It didn't take long for her to become the love of my life.

You are so beautiful to me.

In early nineteen seventy, at the age of thirty five, I had a cardiac arrest. Thanks to God, it happened in a doctor's office across the street from the hospital. After two and a half months in the VA hospital in Martinsburg, it was determined that the cause of that cardiac arrest was a Vegas Reflex. This trigger nerve in the neck manufactures a chemical reaction to stress. After being discharged from the hospital, I played a game of golf with Father Kaiser, and we talked about my future as we played. He thought it was time for me to do something else and get rid of the stress of my current job. He was right.

Chapter Seven
Working for Myself

Sometime soon after my cardiac arrest, I bought a franchise called General Business Services. I would call on small businesses and sell them tax and bookkeeping services. I moved back to Thorp, my wife's hometown, and started my business. I was able to move in with my in-laws while I got the business going. After six months, I was able to move my family back to Wisconsin. We lived above the flower shop, the shop that Joan's mother owned. Joan helped me grow the business and stayed home to raise our family.

It was hard at first – we were back to eating hot dogs and beans. I worked day and night until I finally had offices all over the state of Wisconsin and some in Minnesota. We built a new home on the North Fork River across the river from my in-laws. We lived together in that home for thirty-six years.

Being back in our home state of Wisconsin allowed me to rejoin a favorite pastime, the annual whitetail deer hunt. What a fun get-together! My brother-in-law, Vern; his sons, Scott and Steven; my brother, Charles; his son, Michael; and sometimes grandson, John, were all part of our hunting party. The fun revolved around not just the hunt, but my famous seafood chowder.

PHIL'S SEAFOOD CHOWDER:
½ lb. bacon, diced, browned
1 onion, chopped fine, fry in bacon drippings
4 large potatoes, diced

3 cups of water
Cook potatoes, onions, & bacon in water
approx. 10 mins.
Add the following ingredients:
1 lb. bay scallops
½ lb. shrimp
1 pkg. crab meat
1 pkg. lobster meat
½ lb. cod, cut in cubes
1 - 12oz. can evaporated milk
2 tsp. salt & 1 tsp. pepper
½ tsp. garlic powder
¼ lb. butter
Cook approx. 30 minutes, then add 1 pint
of half and half.
Cook on really low burner or it will
scorch.

Wow, what an awesome meal in the woods. It was probably the real highlight of the hunt.

Back to the grind: One day, one of my GBS clients asked me to find a buyer for its manufacturing business. Joan and I talked about it and thought perhaps we should buy it if it was a good business. We sold all of our GBS businesses and bought it. We were into the manufacturing business. That was nineteen seventy six. We also started building wrought iron railings, manure pumps, and a trash compactor called Trailer-Pac, which we sold throughout North America to such people as Chrysler Corporation, the city of Honolulu, a couple of McDonald's restaurants in Alaska and Kodiak Island, the Dell Webb Corporation at Lake Powell and Lake Mead in Nevada, the Wisconsin DNR, several county park services, and others to numerous to mention.

One of the opportunities I had as owner of this business was to take a business trip to Australia. It was an international engineering conference. I was sponsored by the U.S. Department of Commerce to take our hydraulic manure pump to this engineering show.

The trip started by flying from Minneapolis to Los Angeles, then on to Auckland, New Zealand, Sydney, and then finally landing in Melbourne, Australia. The flight from Los Angeles to Auckland took thirteen hours. We crossed the international dateline and the date and time changed. It took me a day or two to finally get oriented.

I stayed at a very nice place in Melbourne, the Melbourne Hotel. The conference lasted for three weeks. During the conference, I manned a booth and discussed our role in the manufacturing process. I had an opportunity after show hours to visit with folks from several other countries. I thought it would be interesting to talk with people from other cultures, so I brought my tape recorder and recorded a number of our conversations.

I learned so many interesting things during my stay in Australia. I went in July, which is their mid-winter. I learned that on Sundays, all of the businesses shut down because of the football games. Saturday brings people out where they enjoy huge swap meets. I went to a football game and I learned that if they don't like a ref, they run out on the field and beat him up. You're also afforded the opportunity to place bets on scores of players and so forth.

On one of the weekends, I decided to rent a car and drive into the backcountry. I learned to drive on the "wrong side" of the road. It was definitely a challenge. There is no speed limit when you are out of town. It just doesn't exist. The Avis agent told me to "have at it." So I learned that was their way of warning me that there were no speed limits.

One other thing that was quite evident was the number of kangaroo running around. It is similar to our deer population. But the kangaroos come in various sizes, from giants down to tiny ones.

I did happen to stop at a town called Ballarat. It was a very small mining community at one time. It had a significant gold processing plant on the edge of town. Because of the large gold deposits, one can still have fun out there panning for gold in the stream. I found some and brought it back with me. It was challenging because, although it wasn't snowing, it was freezing cold.

I also toured some historic places like the cathedral in Melbourne. I spent an entire day there because it was such an interesting and beautiful place. The intricate workmanship involved in the process of building it all those many years ago was intriguing.

I also found it fascinating to go to the beach, which was fairly deserted. I even found a precious stone. It was an opal, and I brought it back with me too. Australia is famous for its precious stones, especially opals. I took it to a store and the shopkeeper told me it was a triplet opal.

After three weeks, it was good to set out for home. We made a stop in Fiji. It, too, is a very interesting country. It is small, but it looked like paradise. I had the occasion to teach one of the shopkeepers how to make a milkshake at the ice cream shop. The guy didn't have a clue what I was talking about, so I walked him through it. After I made mine, he called all of his buddies and made a bunch for his friends and everybody ended up having milkshakes. Fiji is a very beautiful place.

We went through customs when we entered Hawaii. I spent a lot of time there, as they went through every bag thoroughly. It was the same when I landed in Australia. I spent a lot of time in customs because of this. It was interesting because I saw the sun go down twice during the same flight. When I got back home, it took about three or four days before I knew when to go to bed and when to get up. The jet lag really got to me. All in all, it was a worthwhile trip.

After growing our business, we built a brand new manufacturing plant in nineteen seventy nine. But in nineteen eighty, the dairy business dropped out of sight. We had twenty six employees, welders and assemblers working for us. But the business could only support one employee. We sold that business in nineteen eighty.

Now that I'd sold the business, I was out of work. It didn't take long before a former GBS client and lawyer asked me to do an accounting investigation for him on a criminal case that he was handling. He asked if I knew of a private detective that we could use. That gave me an idea. I checked into the requirements for a Private Detective license and found that I needed to go to school and pass an examination. I went to school in Madison, Wisconsin, took the tests and got my private detective license soon after

It wasn't long before I owned my very own private detective agency. I called it *Surveillance*

Phil's Private Detective License

Unlimited. I concentrated on handling only criminal cases, as they seem to be more in my scope of interest. So for the next five years, I spent my time doing criminal investigations, testifying in court, and working for a number of different entities. Most of my business came from lawyers, banks, insurance companies and a few private individuals. I did get some work from public institutions such as the Division of Criminal Investigations for the State of Wisconsin. Local sheriffs and, sometimes, friends-in-need also called on my services.

If I were to document every one of the cases I worked on over five years, it would fill a book by itself. So, I'm going to relate just a few of the cases to give you a cross-section of the kind of stuff I was involved in.

I only had one employee, a woman named Mary. In the detective business, you need a male and female partner in order to have complete access to a suspect or a subject, and we worked together as a team for quite a while. One day she came to me and told me that she wasn't comfortable anymore with the criminal cases in our business. So, I finally ended up doing all the business myself.

One of the very few non-criminal cases that I took was a civil case. It was for a woman who suspected her husband of having an affair. She wanted photos as proof. So Mary and I did surveillance for several weeks. And indeed, we acquired very revealing photos of the subject actually having sex. We turned those photos over to our client. She paid me very well for that job, and I asked her if there was anything more we could do for her.

She said, "No, I'm just going to go out and buy a new BMW and charge it to my husband." I guess in some cases you call that blackmail, but she decided to keep him, as he owned a large grocery store. With those photos, she realized she could get whatever she wanted from him. From that time on, I only took criminal cases.

I worked on one case for an attorney who represented the father of a woman who was shot to death. Her father suspected it was murder, so I worked for years investigating that case. I remember it well. I had to go up north on Christmas Day, as a matter of fact. The deceased was still in the automobile when I arrived. The murder had happened about eight hours earlier. The woman was shot in the head with a twenty two caliber pistol, owned by her husband. He claimed she committed suicide. She was shot in her car at the end of the driveway of her husband's home; they were separated at the time.

When I got there, there were police officers all over the place. Of course, the authorities didn't want me around, and it took a few days to get a court order to give me access to the crime scene and the evidence. After the crime lab was finished with processing the auto, weapon, body, home and anything else, I had access.

After about a year, we wanted an independent expert to examine the murder weapon. So I went to the county sheriff to pick it up. The evidence locker didn't have the pistol. The sheriff showed me documents that it was in possession of DCI, Division of Criminal Investigation. I drove to Madison, Wisconsin to DCI and they showed me a receipt that it had been returned back to the county sheriff's department. I guess this was one of those cases of following the bouncing ball. I went back to the sheriff's department the next day. The sheriff was really pissed off at me and insisted that the weapon was returned to the possession of DCI.

Now this is when it got really interesting, perhaps a little too interesting and dangerous for me. For some reason, the cops were covering up something and didn't want me stomping around anymore. They set up all kinds of roadblocks to my investigation. They followed me a lot of the time and were just generally being a real pain in the ass. They must have had something to hide.

That's when I went back to DCI and told them what I had found. Then DCI hired me to continue working on the case. Seems as though the sheriff had sold lots of guns over the years, all of them from concluded cases. Apparently, he messed up this time and sold the gun in this active case.

It took a long time, more than a year, but I finally found the gun at a pawnshop in Peoria, Illinois. I finally had my evidence. The end result to this investigation was that the sheriff went to federal prison in Leavenworth, Kansas with a twenty six year sentence. He died in prison. Several others in the sheriff's department resigned or were discharged. The lead detective went to state prison for withholding evidence. He died in prison too. We never got to prove our case because the district attorney never took it to trial. His reasoning was that all of the evidence was tainted. Justice was not served in this case. To this day, I still think the husband of the deceased woman got away with murder.

I had my share of other kinds of cases like burglary, arson, rape, embezzlement, armed assaults, and all of those kinds of things.

Another case was that of an insurance company that hired me to find evidence to support their contention that the controller of a large corporation had embezzled thirty five thousand dollars. He did have a really good scheme. He would write out checks, in small amounts three thousand, four thousand, and five thousand dollars to various bogus contractors to pay for contract work, supposedly. He then sent checks to an address in Menomonee Falls, Wisconsin, which turned out to be the address of his sister.

His sister worked in a bank, where she deposited the checks in separate accounts. She would keep ten-percent of the total and then return the balance to the controller, her brother. It took me a while, but I caught on to him. Soon after, I found out that he bought a new Cadillac for his girlfriend. He paid cash for that Cadillac. All in all, it turned out that he had stolen one hundred seventy thousand dollars, not the thirty five thousand dollars that had originally been suspected.

Then there was the arson to a very large resort in northern Wisconsin. The owner collected a very large insurance check on the loss of property. He paid off the mortgage and walked away with a pocket full of cash. Of course, the owner was in Florida at the time of the fire, which gave him a perfect alibi. When I found out that his seventeen year-old nephew had just bought a brand-new four-wheel drive pickup truck for cash, I knew something was wrong. With a little pressure, I got him to confess to the burning and tell me how his uncle gave him cash to burn down the resort. Criminals are just plain stupid, in most cases anyway.

One of the scariest events I was involved in was a shooting incident that took place on 7th Street in St. Paul, Minnesota. I was hired by an insurance company to try to locate some valuable artwork that was stolen on the east coast. This was one of those times where I worked in conjunction with the authorities, the FBI and some other affiliates. It took quite a while before I was able to track down the people who were involved in the theft, and I tracked them to St. Paul.

On more than one occasion, I was able to do surveillance on those people and found their safe place on 7th Street. While doing surveillance on the subjects one night, all hell broke loose. Several people exited the building firing a bunch of weapons and, little did I know, the FBI was waiting for them. The suspects opened fire, and it sounded like a goddamn war. From my location, I had a difficult time seeing exactly what was going on, but I sure as hell kept my head down. When the smoke cleared, the subjects were all gone except one, whom the FBI had wounded and taken into custody. That was one night I don't ever care to repeat.

Criminals are just plain stupid. They act like criminals and in most cases it's the reason they get caught. A couple of times I had shotguns and other firearms poked in my face, but in each case I got the hell out of there as fast as I could.

Only once, during my entire agency experience, did I have to use my weapon. It was on a drug deal with a very uncooperative subject. I shoved my firearm in his mouth. When he felt the cold steel at the back of his throat, he changed his mind and cooperated. As a matter of fact, he became one of my most important informants.

Once, I was in Jackson, Mississippi for a court hearing. When the defendant entered the courtroom, with bailiff at his side, he somehow got the bailiff's weapon and opened fire inside the courtroom. Now, that made me fill my drawers. When you hear a weapon go off inside a courtroom, it is really, really loud. The guy was subdued and no one got hurt, but it scared the shit out of everybody. Obviously, he did not get his hearing that day.

These are just a few of my stories, though I could go on and on. A good private detective can work 24/7 making a lot of money, but it doesn't take long to get burned out. By mid nineteen eighty six, I was definitely burned out, and I needed to do something different. I learned about a pre-cast concrete company looking for someone to help, so I called and found out that the owner, Joe Wieser, was in Alaska at the time. I saw him the following week at his office in Menomonee, Wisconsin.

Chapter Eight
Our Home by the River

In nineteen seventy, after moving back to Thorp, Joan and I set out to raise our family. We built a home in the country on the banks of the North Fork River. We lived there for over thirty years, raising our family and enjoying the fruits of our labor.

At a very young age, I would go with my family to Canada to fish. I continued the tradition with Joan and the girls. For our families, this is still a major vacation spot. I bought a pickup truck topper as our first camping vehicle. It wasn't long before I traded for a class A motor home, which was a thirty three foot home on wheels. Every year when the kids were out of school, we would go fishing in Canada.

We also took Mary and Leo, Joan's parents. I remember one time when the kids were real small; Suzanne was asleep at the bottom of the boat, and her fishing pole hooked the most fish while she just slept. My mother, Dorothy, was crazy about walleye fishing, and she and my father always made the trip with us too.

Leo and Mary Hedler

Raleigh Lake was where we fished for lake trout, and I got to eat the best blueberry pie in all of Canada.

Early on, we fished on Lac du Malacs, where we caught walleyes like they were going out of style. Year after year, we would return to Rueben's Landing and fish in our favorite spots: Gull Island, Sand Point, Popular Point, and a few spots that we had to name ourselves, such as Birch Island and Rock Ledge Island. Sometimes we would make the trip all the way to Bolton Bay for some really big Northerners. I called them snakes.

After we discovered Basket Lake, we fished there for walleyes from then on. That lake is twenty six miles of very rough road off of Highway seventeen. What a trip. It's a beautiful place, and one time when we went up to the lake, Mary caught a thirteen pound walleye and broke her pole. I have it now, and it hangs on my wall.

Shore Lunch in Canada

Because we always went up there in the early spring, usually mid-May, we had to pack snowmobile suits. There were a lot of times when we had to wear them fishing. All of us, Mom and Dad, Leo and Mary, Joan and the kids really enjoyed shore lunches. We would fillet walleyes and cook them in a cast iron pan over a wood fire. We made our coffee in a can with water from the lake, and it was the best coffee we ever tasted.

Early in our marriage, Joan and I would always go fishing to the Boundary Waters in Canada. Our guide, Frank LaRue, was quite an experienced guide as we portaged in the Boundary Waters. There were boats on several portage locations, and we carried our gear from one to the next and finally found a place where we caught a lot of walleyes and had some great times.

As we traveled and fished together in Canada, a family bond developed that would unite us for the rest of our lives. Even through rain and storms, we found joy in just being there with the campfires, and the sound of the loons on the lakes. Even the black flies were part of the whole experience.

It did seem like all the women, Joan, Mary, Catherine, Suzanne, and Dorothy caught all of the fish. I was generally the guy who operated the motorboat, and Leo and I cleaned all the fish while the women got the rest of the food ready. We ate likes kings and queens. If there ever was a highlight of my family life, this was it. All of the problems of the world seemed to disappear while we were fishing in Canada. In later years, my brother, Charles, was a regular on many of our trips up north. To this day, we still talk about the big ones that got away.

As our children grew up they were strongly influenced by Joan's Polish heritage. Mary's father, Joe Tobola, emigrated from Poland. Their Polish customs infiltrated our family. We particularly enjoyed polka dancing.

We got so involved in Polish customs and music that my children, Catherine and Suzanne, started a polka band. Along with a few other friends, they played for many weddings, anniversaries, and other events around Wisconsin. Their band was called Kasha (which means Catherine in Polish) and the Polka Magic. I would drive them around in my motor home, and when they were finished playing for the evening, they would all sleep on the way home. Playing together and earning some money helped these young people not only learn entrepreneurship, but also the importance of sharing a common bond. What a great way for them to learn some of life's lessons.

To this very day, polka music and dancing are my favorite pastimes. My wife was the best dancer I'd ever known. We spent endless hours at weddings and other polka dances. One of my favorite events is the Polish Fest in Milwaukee, Wisconsin. It is held each June for three days on the lakefront of the Summer Fest grounds. It remains an annual event for me. Now, some of Joan's sisters, their husbands, and her brother and his wife go to the Polish Fest together. Sometimes I see my aunts there too.

Although there are lots of famous polka bands at this event, my favorite band is Jimmy Sturr. His band is so complete; it's a twenty five piece band, and he always makes a point to honor the military veterans too. It is his tribute to the American way of life. His music is unbelievable, and I still go there by myself and remember all of our good times. Besides, I like the food.

Lately, I've been going there on my Harley motorcycle. I usually visit my nephew's family, get my Harley serviced, and just make a big trip of the Polish Fest.

Another thing Joan and I taught our children, Catherine and Suzanne, was to learn to snow ski. Since then, Suzanne's children, Hannah and Neil, have both become addicted to our annual trip out west to ski. We usually head for Big Mountain, in Whitefish, Montana, a paradise for skiers.

My granddaughter, Caitlin, now has her driver's license and her own car. She has become quite a lady.

Cortni has also grown up and is taking Driver's Education now. So, pretty soon she'll have her license. She's quite a young lady, too.

Caitlin

Cortni

Hannah and Neil are both really involved in competitive swimming and are doing a great job.

I can't begin to imagine life without my grandchildren. When I was sick, they were all there watching over Grandpa. They also like Grandpa's cooking. He makes good waffles, and he makes the best dumplings. Grandma, my wife Joan, shaped the characters of these kids. Their kindness is a direct result of their Grandma's teaching. A visit by them reminds me that Joan is still by my side. I see her in my children and grandchildren and will always be thankful for the charmed life I've been given by my family.

The bumps in the road of life are paved over with a hug, a smile, just knowing that a greeting card is always in my mailbox, the four-wheeler rides, fishing in the river, celebrating everyone's birthdays or other parties. We always had the best parties.

My Daughter, Catherine

Catherine, the teacher, has such a love for

music and for the little kids. She's a non-stop talker, and her grooming is not matched by anyone.

My Daughter, Suzanne

Suzanne, the nurse, is a professional. You would want her around when the chips are really down. Her dedication to making you well again is almost superhuman. Both of my daughters' lives are very busy; they have their jobs and families. However, they always have time for me. At the drop of a hat, they are there when needed the most. It's really comforting to know that I am in such good hands.

My son-in-law, John, is a keeper. His dedication to his family makes me very proud. He is a Physician's Assistant and is the ultimate professional dedicated to his job. Suzanne is so fortunate to have this man, John Voros.

John Voros

Life is not without trials. However, all the good things far outweigh the bad. Have faith! My wife was the influence in the strengthening of my faith. Whenever things got tough, her soft touch and gentle voice of reassurance, which I heard even in what was not spoken, allowed God to intervene. Her handiwork is everywhere in my life. From the quilts on my bed to the recipe box in the kitchen to the children and grandchildren; she is always present.

You are so beautiful.

God held Joan and I together physically for forty eight years, and keeps us together forever.

Chapter Nine
Come Fly with Me

I can't even remember all of the airplanes that I've owned and flown, but who cares? I have been plane-crazy my entire life. I got my pilot's license while we lived in Voorheesville, New York. It was the first time I could afford to earn a license, though I'd been flying with my father since I was a youngster.

One day my flight instructor said, "Okay Phil, are you ready to solo today?" As he got out of that Aeronca Champ, I wondered if I was truly ready.

As I lined up for takeoff, my mind raced through all of the training thoughts, and I climbed out over the lake at the end of the airstrip. I shouted out, as this was my first ride by myself. I felt a certain sense of calm for the first few minutes, and then I came back to reality – to the fact that I would have to do everything myself and do it right, including landing this airplane. It was all under my control.

The landing wasn't pretty, but I got it on the ground. What a feeling! In the office, they cut off my shirttail and hung it on the wall as a symbol of my first solo flight. I continued training, which led to a private pilot's license. I did the flight tests in a Piper Tri-Pacer. I remember a few of the airplanes that I owned; that one nineteen sixty three Cessna 172, what a beautiful aircraft! And all of the airplanes that followed were beautiful. I'm still plane-crazy.

Starduster Too

Citabria

Cessna 172

I built a kit plane, an Avid Catalina, and sold it to my friend, Bjorn Ronjom, and the aircraft is now in the country of Norway. I now have a Cessna 177 Cardinal, Stardust II Biplane and the J-3 Cub, like my father owned long ago. I'm also building a Titan II S, which is a high wing pusher. Building these aircraft is what I do as my pastime.

J-3 Cub

With an airstrip in my backyard for over thirty five years, flying has been a central part of my life. It is used for business and pleasure. The skies have been very friendly to me, giving Young Eagle flights, flying to EAA in Oshkosh, and just going up for a few minutes. Sometimes I would fly over to Steve's place, my flying buddy, or over to Bob Merrick's. The joy of flying is hard to describe; it has to be felt.

A few trips have provided some unusual moments. I flew Rich Boie and Brian Van Ert out to Rocky Mountain, North Carolina one day in early spring. On one of the fuel stops, we were on top of a mountain in western West Virginia. The crosswinds were really bad, and after we landed and taxied to the fuel pumps, Rich got out and kissed the ground. From there on back to Neillsville, Wisconsin the trip was uneventful, until we got about ten miles south of the airport. All of a sudden a spring snowstorm came over, and lo and behold, we were in the thick of it. But wouldn't you know, the skies opened up directly over the airport. We landed, and it started snowing again; we could hardly see through the snow to find the terminal building.

Then there was the time I flew Dave Haas to Akron, Ohio one Saturday morning, so he could attend an equipment auction. When he finished the auction, we flew back, and he asked me to drop him off in Marshfield before 6:30 p.m. He wanted to watch his son, Steve, race stockcars there. Dave did it all in one day. Flying your own aircraft is the only way to get around.

Most recently, I flew a Cessna 172 that belonged to Duffy Guyer to Texas on a business trip. I picked up Andy Wieser in Redwing, Minnesota and a building contractor, Mike, in Iowa. By the time we got to Texas, it was dark. Andy learned a lot about flying that day, and on the way back, I let him do most of the flying. I fell asleep, but when I heard the engine starting to run rough and sputter, that kind of woke me up. The carburetor had filled with ice, so I quickly took control of the aircraft. After I applied heat to the carburetor, everything was fine as we flew back to Wisconsin.

That day was the real start of Andy's interest

in flying. I am proud to say that I had a part in his becoming a private pilot. Andy took flying lessons and is now a licensed pilot.

All in all, in over fifty years of flying, I never had an incident, even though there were times I was happy that God was sitting next to me. Good training, attention to details, and commitment made for a safe and dependable flying career.

Now, flying into the EAA (Experimental Aircraft Association) in Oshkosh, Wisconsin each year for their annual event is a pilot's dream come true. It's not for novice pilots at all; the discipline required will test every bit of your physical and mental skills. This is the busiest airport in the world during the fly-in. My friends, Steve, Bob, and I fly to EAA every year. We camp out next to our aircraft since that's the only accommodation available. There are no other places to stay. We walk the grounds for two or three days, stopping at hundreds of booths to learn and sometimes buy more aviation stuff. Even non-fliers can have a great time at Oshkosh. Aircraft from around the world are there. The daily air shows make for pure enjoyment.

I hope to pass on this tradition to my only grandson, Neil Voros. All of my grandchildren like to fly, but Cortni is especially fond of going up with Grandpa. Hannah, Neil and sometimes Caitlin will go for a ride when the time is right.

And I know that at least two of my Young Eagles became pilots, Beth Wytula and Craig Alger.

Every flight is a new adventure. Come fly with me and you will know firsthand the freedom of landing in a soybean field or a freshly cut hayfield. I have flown for both business and pleasure, and if you want to know the real meaning of freedom and beauty, and most of all faith, become a pilot. All of these great flying machines make my work feel like playtime, and they save a lot of travel time too. I go directly to the customer's farms and home again. No bridges to cross, no construction delays in the wild blue yonder. It doesn't end there; the joy of flying is also hangar talk among pilots and non-pilots alike. I know what's in store for me in heaven when it's time for my final flight.

Chapter Ten
Starting Over

By mid nineteen eighty six, this fifty year old man was burned-out, and I knew that I had to do something different. I learned about this company selling pre-cast concrete that was looking for someone to help. So I called and found out that Joe Wieser was in Alaska, but I could see him at his office in a week. I met Joe Wieser at his office in Menomonee, Wisconsin in mid-August nineteen eighty six. We talked for a while, and when we finally ran out of things to say, I said, "Joe, I'm going to go work for you."

He said, "What are you going to do?"

I said, "I'm going to sell pre-cast concrete."

He asked me how much it was going to cost him to have me work for him, and I said,

"Nothing, because I would make my money from his profits on the job."

He asked me when was I planning to start, and my answer was "Next week."

So on August twenty sixth, nineteen eighty six, I went to work with his team, and I've never looked back. I just celebrated twenty-three years with the company. I've been made part of their family. Joe retired, but his sons, Andy, Mark, and Dan, took over. And they, too, are not just my employers, but my friends.

Over the years, I sold commercial, highway, and agriculture, but as we grew, I now sell agricultural products. My journey over the last several years has taken me throughout the U.S. and even over to the Netherlands. I was and am known as Mr. Tradeshow. Working at all of these tradeshows over the years has given me a chance to meet and make friends with many people. I met tradeshow exhibitors, customers and others along the way. They are all important to me, and I know that our friendships will last forever.

Speaking of friends, everyone knows that Whitey Eiting (Roger) and I are inseparable. He's my best friend, as is Kathleen Friedel. Linda; Denise; Marty; Larry; Jon; Amy; Andrew; Beth; Bill; Bjorn; Rich; Brian; Renee; Tiffany; Tom; Howard; Molly; Josie; Lynn and her sisters, Kim and Kelly; Tracy; Sandy and Chuck; Mike; Jack;

Deb and Lori; Don; Doug; Ed; Frank; Joe and Gloria; Jeff and Kim; Jennifer; Jenny; Jana; Dan; Kim; Kelly; Marlene and Dennis; Sheri and Lisa; Marsha; Mary; Nels and Matt; John and Kim; The Reagan; Frank and Mary; Roger; Roman and Todd; Ron; Dan; Todd; Shelly; Cheri; Steve; Tom and Darla; Patty; Mike; Erin; Kay; Joan and Keith; Jim and Joan: there are so many friends and neighbors. It's too hard to name them all.

One is really special: Kay Anderson, who recently passed away. She was a very good friend of mine for a very long time. She had an unfortunate accident on March seventh two thousand and eight. Kay was that special person who always had a special smile. She worked for a power company in western Iowa and brought brightness to every room she entered. She was a regular at every tradeshow and worked really hard. I miss that woman, and my heart goes out to her family.

Mike is my buddy from Iowa Development Corporation; that guy can inspire you to do better. He always stands tall and always has kind words for everyone.

My friend, Dan, is one of our drivers and is also a very good friend of mine. We hunt together and talk on a regular basis. He always encourages me to sell more, which makes my life more fun.

I keep in touch with my Aunt Josephine by

phone; my Aunt Zama and Uncle Ken; my Aunt Ruth; my cousins in California, Gwen, Elizabeth and Bill; and the many more relatives are a big part of my life too.

Some more of the people that I've known through all our farm show days are Deb and Lori. These two women have been my friends for probably twenty years. We've shared lots of laughs, a few beers, and just generally hung out together. One of the things I learned from these two ladies, is to make sure that they are never allowed into your motel room alone. If you do, you will find Fruit Loops in your bed. Deb and I have remained good friends for all these years and she is not just smart but beautiful. Deb is a woman with unique courage, even when she is hurting, she inspires other's, she is a keeper.

I could go on for a very long time. All of these people have had an impact on my life, and I'm sure I've missed a lot of folks, but this is a sample of the people in my life to show the impact they made on me and how they've gotten close to me over the years.

And here's a little more detail on Whitey: I'll never forget the moment I met him. It was at a Green Bay Farm show. We set up outside in the tradeshow parking lot, where the Reich center is now. We had three side-by-side lots: R&J, Dairy Tile, owned by Whitey; Wrightstown

Manufacturing, owned by Jack, another special guy; and me, in the Wieser Concrete booth. Anyway, I heard this guy, Roger Eiting, standing in the booth next to me. He was giving a sales pitch to some prospects. Since I wanted to learn more, I stood close enough to overhear what he had to say. I thought at the time that it was a really good sales pitch. He talked about the way he installed tiles on the walls of modern dairy farms.

I heard him say, "Sir, the biggest benefit to you is that these tiles that I install are absolutely unbreakable." And just then he bumped into a tile, and it dropped down and broke into a hundred pieces. Then he looked down, and without missing a beat, went on to explain that he always brought competitors' tiles to the show in case that would happen so that he could show how bad his competitors' tiles were. He said "You might pay a little more for tiles from me, but you will get the best tile. And that will never happen to you."

I had to walk away; I was laughing so hard, I almost wet my pants. It was during that chance meeting that I learned that the way to tell when Whitey is lying is when his lips are moving. Later that night, Jack, Whitey, and I had some beer together at the Midway Hotel – perhaps a bit too much beer.

That is when our friendship of over twenty years began. Whitey is a great person. I don't mean tall or big, I mean he's the kind of person that would give you the shirt off his back. He would not come to get you out of jail. No, he would be sitting right beside you saying, "Well, Miller, we really screwed up this time." Everyone should be fortunate enough to have Whitey as a friend. His wife, Janice, and daughter, Missy, and all his family are awesome people. I thank God that he brought us together. Whitey is a big NASCAR and Packer fan. I could write a complete story on just those things. In fact, I could write a book on just our friendship alone.

Everything we've done together over the years has been done because we love and respect one another. No doubt God wants us to live our lives the way we do, but I'll bet even God shakes his head sometimes. You need to know this man, and one of the things about him is that he passes the most deadly farts known to man. He can clear a room in an instant. In fact, if he were sent to Iraq, the war would end the day he arrives. And every country around would cry, "Foul" at America's new Weapon of Mass Destruction.

We both have learned to live our lives fully. When people say that we are a couple of mischievous guys, I don't think it would be an accurate description of us. Have we ever grown up to full adulthood? I don't think so. I do know that when we die, we will probably spend a lot of time in purgatory. When we do arrive at the gates of heaven, God himself will greet us, looking somewhat disbelieving, with a tablet in hand – not with a listing of our good works or misdeeds on earth, but with a schedule of farm shows we'll work in heaven for all of eternity.

If you want to learn what PMA is, Positive Mental Attitude, then stick around us for just a day, as our mission on earth is to be a friend to everyone and make him or her laugh, and even through the toughest speed bumps, cry with them when they need compassion. Our major theme in life is *Dance like no one is watching, Love like you've never been hurt, and work like you don't need the money.* We do remember yesterday, but we don't look back. We don't look too far ahead either, as today is our day. If we are not together in person, we talk on the phone all the time. Who do you think came to my home to celebrate my seventy-second birthday. You got it. It was Whitey and Jack. It was a Saturday night, and boy was it ever a Saturday night!

As I said earlier, Whitey is a huge NASCAR fan. He worked in the pits for years on a NASCAR team with car owner, Richard Childres, and racecar driver, Dave Marcus, a Wisconsin driver. To this day, Whitey can be found in Bristol, Daytona, Talladega, Martinsville, Las Vegas, Texas speedway, Chicago, and Milwaukee during one of their auto events. However, whenever the races are on, they better not coincide with the Green Bay Packer's schedule. Because you see, Whitey is also a season ticket holder.

You might know that when I wanted six tickets to the Christmas Day two thousand ands five, Chicago Bears game against the Green Bay Packers, I got the tickets from Whitey. Kathleen, who was born in Chicago, is, of course, a Bears fan, and I had to go to the game. Yes, I remember the Bears lucked out and won that game.

Then there was the time when I was working the World Dairy Expo in Madison. On a Thursday evening, late at night, Whitey called and said that he would not be in the area as he and his camper were in Talladega, Alabama for the race.

I said, "What the hell are you doing there? Aren't you a little early? The race is Sunday."

And his answer was odd but true, "We have a great parking spot." It is his way of spontaneity.

Then there was the time we worked the Farm Progress Show in Lancaster, Wisconsin and our hotel was in Dubuque, Iowa. So driving back to the hotel one evening, we stopped in Dickeyville, Wisconsin. We stopped in at Kupper's Bar for a cold one, and when we entered, there were only a few patrons. We chatted with the bartender, just small talk. In walks these older women; I would say they were in their late seventies or eighties. Whitey greeted them with "Ladies, what's happening? Is it recess at the nursing home?"

And I think one of them said to him, "Yeah, sonny, you want to dance?"

Anyway, that broke the place up. There was a guy next to me who answered his cell phone, and I heard him say, "No honey, I won't be home for supper. I'm sure I'm going to be late. I'm at Kupper's and I'm not leaving, as I've never laughed so hard at these two guys from Farm Progress. I'll be home when they leave."

The word must have spread throughout the town, as in fifteen minutes the place was packed. Whitey worked the crowd, just like a pro. I think we closed the bar. The guy with the cell phone never left.

The bartender said to us, "Maybe I should hire you guys to come in every week, as I've never had so much business."

The Exhibitor's Diner was in Platteville, Wisconsin. We agreed to give our friends, Renee and Tiffany, a ride to the diner. Both have been the best of friends to us for years. And while we were standing in the food line, I heard someone say, "Hey, it looks like those two goofy bastards over there." And without missing a beat, Whitey looked at me and said, "Philly, they must be talking about you and me."

We met one time in the Minneapolis airport. Whitey came in on a flight from Green Bay, Wisconsin, and I took the limo shuttle from Eau Claire. We were flying to Las Vegas, Nevada and planned to rent a car from there and drive to the Tulare Farm Show in Tulare, California. When we arrived in Las Vegas, I got the car, and Whitey said, "Miller get me to the Union Plaza downtown as soon as possible."

Well, on the way to the Plaza, some guy ran a red light and almost hit us. It is one of the few times in my life that I've ever been scared. And Whitey said, "Miller, you damn near got us killed."

And I said, "I'm glad he was coming on your side of the car."

At the Union Plaza, we went to the sports booking section and Whitey plunked down seven hundred or eight hundred dollars on the following weekend's Daytona 500 race. We stuck around and gambled for a while, then took off for California. Actually, we stayed at Whiskey Pete's in Prim, Nevada. It is at the California/Nevada border. On Sunday morning, we left early, and we didn't get more than two miles down the road, and I had to stop the car and bail out. Whitey had let off one of his deadly discharges, and it smelled like a dead animal that had been in the hot sun for two days.

We stopped in Barstow, California to attend

Mass. Of course, our luck was that it was a Spanish mass. We didn't really understand anything, but the music was good. The trip across the desert was punctuated with lots of stops to air out the car and, as Whitey said, "Philly, you'd think with a brand new car like this one they would use better paint on the engine, because it really stinks when it's burning the paint off, don't you think?"

I can tell you one thing, the second renter of this car is in for a surprise, because there is no way in hell they are going to get the smell out of there and make it smell fresh again. We must have stopped fifty times; I should have had him walk.

At the Tulare Farm Show grounds, we met up with Dan Kempf, our Wieser truck driver. We spent two days setting up our booth and getting everything in place. It took about five minutes for Dan and Whitey to become friends, and the three of us went to supper that night. It was a really good place called Apple Annies on Highway 99 and Prosperity Avenue. When we finished eating, we asked the waitress where we could get a beer. She said that her daughter and son-in-law had a place called CC's (Chuck and Charlene's) not far away. It was a nice little place with a couple of pool tables and a dance floor. It wasn't long before Whitey and Dan got into a game of pool. I remember Chuck telling me that the next guy to play the winner was the best player in all of Tulare

County, if not the best in the Central Valley.

Well, Dan disappeared for few minutes and then came back and stood in the doorway with his own pool cue, and I thought, "Holy shit, this could be serious." We stayed there for hours, while Dan proceeded to kick ass with everyone who stepped up to the table, including Augie, the champion of the region. Needless to say, I didn't drink much beer, as I spent the night looking over my shoulder once word got out that some out-of-towner was kicking ass at CC's.

When Whitey came back from the bathroom, he said to me, "Philly, did you see those urinals in there? They are mounted on the wall, but they mounted them real low. Do you suppose that they knew that there might be somebody like me who needed them low, so that me and my Johnson didn't hang in the water?"

I said, "They did it so that when you are a little wobbly, and you're peeing while on your knees, you can still reach the urinal."

Meanwhile, Dan was still the king of the pool table. When we finally closed the place, and Whitey had a few too many *Miller High Life's*, we were walking across the parking lot, and he said to me, "Philly, do you want me to drive?"

And I said, "No Whitey, I will just be happy if you can walk all the way to the car."

Our week at the tradeshow went very well. Our plan was to drive back to Las Vegas on Sunday. Of course, again we went to Mass on that Sunday morning, and it was a Spanish Mass. I knew it was, but it was a surprise to Whitey. As we knelt down, I saw Whitey reach forward. There was a young lady with her dress caught in her butt, and Whitey was going to pull it out. I grabbed his hand before he was able to do so. After church I asked him what the hell he was thinking.

He looked at me and said, "That looked awful uncomfortable, so I thought I would help her out."

Back at the motel, Whitey had to watch the Daytona 500. Of course, there was three hours' difference between the east and the west coast, so it was early for us to watch it. As soon as it was over, we left for Las Vegas.

Again he said, "Get me to the Union Plaza as soon as possible, so I can collect my winnings." He told me he had won a small fortune.

Now it is three hundred fifty miles across the desert, so it wasn't a real quick trip to the Union Plaza, but when we got there, he went directly to the cashier. He plopped down a big, two-inch high stack of betting tickets. The cashier took them and ran them through the machine and promptly paid Whitey twenty-five dollars. He stood there with a look on his face and his mouth wide open. The cashier asked if there was anything further he could do for him. Whitey said, "No," and as we walked away, I heard him mumble, "Oh my math must have been bad."

The Bateman family, of Elberta, Utah, is a perfect example of customers who grow into friends. Sons Lance, Steve, Jason, Rich and their father, Howard, became our customers long ago. My very good friend Dan, our Wieser boom truck operator, and I have both hunted for Mule deer there at the Bateman Farm. The Bateman farm is sixty miles south of Salt Lake City and has six thousand cows; it is no small feat to keep it all together. Driving onto the farm gives you a feeling for what the West was like in days gone by – big open spaces, foothills leading to rugged mountains, with lots of irrigation systems to grow crops in an area that receives little rain. Can you even imagine handling in excess of twenty to forty newly born calves every day, milking six thousand cows three times a day? Or feeding and tending to that many cows, as well as growing and harvesting thousands of acres of crops? Having a well-oiled machine is the key to their success.

So, one day, Dan and I took a trip to Utah and didn't know what was in store for us. I was just recovering from heart bypass surgery and was not really strong yet, but we arrived at the

Bateman farm a day before the start of hunting. Jason, an avid hunter, showed us around. He couldn't hunt, as he hadn't received a permit, so he was our scout. The area was really big, so we zeroed in on two favorite spots, the apple orchard and an area down by the lake. We posted on the west fringe of the orchard, and there were deer on the east end. There were a lot of does, and after they moved, a very large buck came right at Dan. We waited and waited as it came into very close range. I heard Dan shoot at it, and I also opened fire from afar. That big buck jumped a very high wire fence, and despite guns ablaze, it took off without a scratch.

Our scouting down by the lake paid off, though. Just above the sagebrush, there was a rack. Dan and I both jumped out of the truck and opened fire. After twenty or thirty shots, we bagged a small three-point. It was not what we were after, but we didn't get skunked.

Dan and I have grown to be good friends. We talk by phone on a regular basis. We think alike and, yes, we're from the old school that teaches that hard work and commitment to getting the job done earn the customer's trust.

A few years back, I was invited by a businessman from Holland to work a trade show in the Netherlands. It was in a town called Zwolle. I flew from Minneapolis to Amsterdam in nine and a half hours. A friend with whom I was to work at the trade show picked me up in Amsterdam. I came a few days early, so we could travel through the country. Over the weekend, we went to Belgium and Germany. We stayed at bed and breakfasts a number of times. It was quite interesting. We each got a small room with a shower. In the morning we had breakfast, which was hard-boiled eggs, cold ham, cheese and toast. One of the interesting things was in the evening, when we came back; the proprietor had a pony of beer. I talked to him about it, and he said, "It's a common practice." He was a retired teacher who merely wanted to break even on his enterprise. That is why it was so inexpensive to stay there.

I worked the show for a week. I met many interesting folks. My intention was to convince dairy farmers from the Netherlands to come to the United States, specifically Wisconsin. We toured the farms in many interesting parts of the Netherlands. They had slatted barns, and their houses were actually attached to the front of the barns. There were even barns in the town.

The dairy industry in Holland is subject to a strict quota and manure management laws. So, there are a lot of young people who inherit their farms, sell them and move to Canada or the United States.

One thing I found fascinating in the

Netherlands was that their transportation is by a system of canals. The country is below sea level, so there are canals all over to deal with the rising tidewater. Whenever you are going down the canal on your boat and come upon a bridge, one of the neighbors, who live nearby, goes out and pulls a counterweight to open the bridge so the boat can pass through. He then waits until the boat passes and reactivates the counterweights for the bridge to go back down to accommodate the road traffic.

Another thing I found interesting was that when you go to the grocery store for some goodies, you have to bring your own shopping bag. Most people there carry a cloth bag into the store. I noticed it, but what it was for didn't dawn on me. I waited for quite some time before I realized I needed to stuff the things in my pockets and carry it in my arms.

And yet another thing that was noticeable was that in the Netherlands, there are no school buses. The children must find their own way to school. Most of them ride their bicycles. There are bicycles everywhere, and even the children, some of whom are disabled, don't have special buses. Their parents have to take them to school, or they have to use public transportation. Most of the automobiles were small. Gasoline was about six or seven dollars a gallon there.

Cameras monitor the traffic laws. So if you

break the law, speeding or running red light, your violation is recorded on a camera, and you get a ticket in the mail. Most of the police are heavily armed with automatic weapons. The country is ruled with an iron fist. At the airport in Amsterdam they police in a Gestapo-like manner. There are armed guards everywhere. No one can even cross the street from the parking lot without an airline ticket. They keep the entire airport sanitized. There won't be any terrorists boarding airplanes in Amsterdam.

One day, while working in the trade show, this lady walks up to me and said, "So, you're Phil Miller."

It turned out that she was a transplant from Holland who lived on a farm in Neillsville, Wisconsin, some thirty miles from my home. Here we were, running into one another on the other side of the world. We actually flew back on the same plane. So, traveling has been interesting; sometimes you find a common thread when you least expect it.

Chapter Eleven
One Moment in Time

Ibuilt an airplane, an Avid Catalina, and sold it to a gentleman from Norway who lives in Fort Lauderdale, Florida in the winter months. As part of the deal, I agreed to haul it to Florida. He offered to provide accommodations for me to stay there for two days as payment for transportation. I built a large crate-on a trailer to haul this aircraft. The airplane was fully assembled, except the wings were off, but I got everything to fit. I asked Joan to ride there with me, as I was going to leave the following Friday. This was early April two thousand and four. She said it was too long of a trip, and she didn't want to spend all of that time on the road. She knew that I wouldn't stay there long and would want to turn around and come right back.

When I came home that Thursday night from selling, there were some bags packed by the front door. When I asked her what was wrong, she said that she decided to go along with me to keep me company. So the following Friday we left on our trip. Along the way, we had some trouble with wheel bearings. I got those fixed in Janesville, Wisconsin. On we went to Florida, with no further mishaps. When we arrived in Fort Lauderdale, the nicest fellow greeted us. His name was Bjorn Ronjom; he was a former airline pilot.   He provided us with a nice little condo stocked with beer and food, and we moved right in. We stayed there for the next several days. We took the airplane over to a shipper and put it inside a container. He wanted the trailer too, but it wouldn't fit, so I had to haul it back to Wisconsin. We stayed there for a week and had the best time.

When we finally left, some guy in Georgia ran into our trailer and broke an axle. I was glad it was empty! We had to stop and get it fixed and then set out on our way. Joan was upset about the accident, but it was already over, so it didn't really matter. We then meandered on through Georgia, Tennessee and Kentucky. I remember we went to church in Kentucky; in fact, it was Easter Sunday. It was a really beautiful church. Then we ambled home through Indiana, Illinois and finally home on the banks of the North Fork River.

Sunday, April eighteenth, two thousand and four was by far the worse day of my life. Joan and I went to church in the morning, and during the day, we just hung out around the house. Later that afternoon, the wind was starting to blow things around. So Joan asked me to fasten the door on the gazebo, as the wind was blowing it open. I went to the garage and got a nail and nailed the door shut. When I went back into the house, I walked to the hallway where I saw that the basement door was open. I shouted down the stairs that I had gotten the gazebo door nailed shut. There was no answer, but I never thought anything about it.

As I was getting a drink of water at the kitchen sink, I looked out the window and noticed that one of the largest trees; a huge pine tree in the backyard was broken off probably twenty feet above the ground near the riverbank. For whatever reason, I ran downstairs to find Joan. Since I had no answer, I ran down to the riverbank and there she was; she had been struck by the tree and was pinned under a very large limb. I felt for a pulse, and she barely had one. I ran up and called 911, got my chainsaw from the garage, and cut the tree. I got the limb off of her. It was about that time that the paramedics arrived. I knew right then; things were really, really bad. The paramedics attended to her and took her to

Stanley, Wisconsin hospital where the Flight-for-Life helicopter picked her up and took her to St. Joseph's hospital in Marshfield, Wisconsin. Janet and Brian took me to Marshfield where my daughters were waiting. I knew that the news would not be good. She had massive injuries that were not reversible. She passed away at eleven o'clock that evening.

How could this be? How could this have happened? There are only a few things that I can recall from those next few days. I had lost my lifetime partner in a freak accident. It was almost beyond belief.

I've tried to remember the names and faces of all those people who came to the wake and funeral. It is just impossible to recall. In fact, I don't remember much about those days, but I do remember one thing.

I went to the funeral parlor early on the day of the funeral. When I walked in, there stood Roman Malecha, a friend of mine who lives on the west side of Minnesota. It was probably nine a.m., and there he stood, all by himself, paying tribute to my wife, whom he had never met. He is my friend.

All of those people, my friends and coworkers, to my shock, my surprise, were there, as well as lots of exhibitors from tradeshows, customers John and Kim Pagel, my friends, Janice, Whitey, Kathleen, and the daughters of the

Regans, Sheri and Lisa. I was just stunned to see so many people, and I had no idea of the depth of their compassion.

For the next six months or so, I was a hermit. I locked myself in the house and did some work, often on the phone. I had never been alone. I did not know how to clean and cook and wash clothes. All of the things I took for granted were now really big things in my life. How would I live without this person in my life? This woman I had lived with for almost forty-eight years? Her life snuffed out in an instant. I never got to say good-bye. Probably the hardest part of my loss is the inability to tell her once in a while how much I love her.

I'm not sure when I came out of my shell, but I remember I was down in Iowa selling. On returning home on a Friday night, I saw a sign on Highway H that was lit up. It was a bar called the Corner Pub. I said to myself, "I think I need a beer." So I stopped in. The place was packed, and as I drank my beer, the bartender, a dark-haired, very pretty young lady looked at me, and I sort of looked at her and had this strange feeling. After I drank my beer and ordered another, I said to her, "Would you happen to know Chuck and Sandy Moore?" They were former GBS clients of mine, way back when.

She said, "Yes I know them. They are my parents, and as a matter of fact, they're standing right over there."

She looked somewhat like her mother, which is what reminded me of her parents. Her name was Tracy. Of course when I knew her parents, she was a very young girl.

I went over to them, and we had a long talk.

As the years moved forward, I came to understand that I needed to live alone. To this very day, I still think of my wife every day, but I don't think of the tragedy anymore. I think of all of the good times we had together, and those good times far outweigh that one moment in time. After reading and thinking, I now understand that the only person we know forever is ourselves. So I've come to accept the loss of my wife and have come to know that I have been given the greatest blessing in the world, and that was to have her as my life partner. No one can remove from my being the memories of our life together, the good times. Even some of those bumps in the road seem quite insignificant in the grand scheme of our life together.

Her gravestone is a large granite stone that I took from her rock garden. I didn't have it polished. I had it engraved with her birth and death and there's a little quilt etched on her side and an airplane on mine. It is a natural stone, so different than everything else, but it fits her perfectly. There was only one Joan Catherine (Hedler) Miller, and she will be my wife forever.

Joan Catherine Miller, Deceased April 18, 2004

Chapter Twelve
People

After the death of my wife, Joan, I did not function very well for the first year or two. I was lost without my life partner, but her gentle hand and her Polish "can-do" spirit will forever guide me.

Not wanting to look out my kitchen window at that fatal spot, I built a new home across the river, next to the North Fork airstrip. This place I called "The Salty Dog." When Joan and I were in Alaska a few years prior, we went to Homer, Alaska, a town on the very tip of the Keni Peninsula, at the end of the Spit. There was a very small log cabin tavern called The Salty Dog, and we carved our initials in the wall, along with thousands who had done the same before us.

Naming my new home the "The Salty Dog" was a tribute to my wife.

After building one airplane for Bjorn of Norway, we became great friends, and I still visit him, along with my children and grandchildren, at the Holiday Isle Yacht Club in Fort Lauderdale, Florida. Bjorn and I went to the Sun and Fun Fly-In EAA in Lakeland, Florida in two thousand six. What fun we had! We went again in two thousand seven.

I always stay with my nephew Mike and his wife Lisa for a few days in St. Cloud, Florida. We have a very special bond, which makes us the envy of others, as together we have great fun and cherish each other's special moments. I shall always treasure the times I've spent with them. Their little guy, Christopher, sticks to me like glue. He is such an awesome little guy and is the pot of gold at the end of the rainbow.

The story of how I met another special person in my life, Kathleen, is a dozy. It was the Saturday before Farm Progress Days to be held in Eden, Wisconsin. Although I'm not sure, I believe it was nineteen ninety six. Joan and I had gone to Catherine's home to help around the house. I was cleaning the leaves out of the gutters, standing on a ladder, which was propped against the gutter. For whatever reason, the ladder slipped, and I fell back onto the driveway below and landed on a big flowerpot.

Joan called to the neighbor to dial 911. The ambulance arrived and transported me to the Marshfield, Wisconsin, St. Joseph's Hospital emergency room. The doctor looked at me and said I was either going to surgery to have my spleen removed, or I was going to go home. After several tests throughout the night, I was going home, with lots of pain pills.

The following Monday, I left for Farm Progress Days. I didn't do any of the setup, as I was in no shape. I shouldn't even have been there, but I had Whitey to look after me.

That night, as we entered the Holiday Inn for some food and drink, I had a back spasm and fell flat on my face on the floor. That's when I met Kathleen, as she was the bar and restaurant manager. She came to my side with the concern and caring that only a mother has in her possession. I was okay, I thought. But later I had to go to the Fond du Lac Hospital emergency room to get some more pain pills.

Kathleen was really worried, and we talked for a long time. I convinced her I was okay. We talked about Farm Progress Days, and she said she was working at a church food stand for the Catholic Church and invited me to join her. I told her I would eat there. There was something so caring about this beautiful mother of four children;

she instantly became my friend. I asked her to keep in touch, as it's not often you find a friend that has such a caring heart.

As the years have gone by, I have enjoyed the same close relationship with her as I have had with Whitey. At the funeral of Joan, it was Whitey and Kathleen standing there together, side-by-side, at my side. Kathleen is the kind of person who thinks of everyone else before herself. I thought so much of her that I helped her get a job at Wieser Concrete in the Fond du Lac office. Our customers just love her, and she is the best customer relations person I have ever met.

Kathleen and I went skiing in Montana and vacationed in Florida. Whenever I can, we talk on the phone. Her boys went deer hunting with me, and I enjoyed every minute of it. She will be my friend forever, even though she in only forty six years old. We have this special relationship and understand that we will never marry. But that doesn't matter. We were meant to share one another's life together in a very special way, with kindness and respect for each other. This Chicago girl is special: a Bear's fan. One afternoon, we went to a Green Bay Packer's game – what the hell is wrong with me?! We watched and waited in our hotel after the game for three hours, yes, three hours for what she calls "the best damn pizza she ever had." Of course, the Bears won the game on a fumble. Yes, I have learned to keep away from Lambeau Field.

The one thing that makes Kathleen so special is the fact that she makes a person's heart smile. She always has a cheerful word, is a good listener, and when things get tough, she makes your life feel good again. She will always be my friend. I could go on and on, page after page, and give thousands of reason to like this woman, but kindness is the one word that defines her being.

I met Linda several years ago at a farm show. The spark in her eyes cannot be overstated, and she is also a beautiful woman. We have become very close friends over the years. Linda has always been there for me. Her word is as good as gold. Her business skills are absolutely fantastic. She spent most of her time in the Tomah, Wisconsin office, but was chosen to move to California to start up a new manufacturing facility in Tulare, California. She did it by herself. If I wanted someone on the other end of the rope to save my life, it would be Linda. How do you describe caring, commitment, and charm? It's Linda.

Denise is a rock, a very kind and gentle person. I can always find comfort when I think of Denise. She and I have worked together for more years than I can remember. A hug from Denise is just like winning the lottery; it makes for a very rich life.

Marty is one of those friends who just comes into your life and seems to talk about business and personal things as if we grew up together and never kept secrets. Marty and her husband, Tony, and their son, Alex, live in Madison and help me at the drop of a hat. Marty loves to fly in the J-3 Cub. A few years ago, during a Farm Progress show in Bloomer, Marty and I took a flight over the Farm Progress to prove I was working there. I threw a box of business cards out.

Marty and I have had lots of fun together. This young woman is someone who can turn your dark day into light. Marty is one of those friends who are with you, always. Nothing is too personal to discuss with her. She's one of the best listeners you could ever find, and a beautiful woman too. Out of the blue, a call will come in from Marty just because she is concerned for her friends. Her smile will really get to you; it helps brighten up your day.

One day, I wandered into the Thorp Dairy Bar. A young woman had reopened it. I immediately found their food to be awesome. There was no longer a reason for me to cook for myself anymore. I eat there regularly.

It didn't take long for me to befriend the young woman who reopened the Thorp Dairy Bar, Kristi. This woman really knows home cooking at it's best. Kristi and I have become great friends over the last few years. She has three children; in fact, Kayla, her oldest daughter does all of my mowing for me. Hayley, her other daughter, and I are close too. We spend time together. Kristi has this internal sense, she knows me pretty well after a few years. Sometimes she brings her kids to the "Salty Dog" for a cookout, and we just sit around and talk. She's really easy to get along with and always seems to have concern for my health and well-being. She is such a nice person, a friend right up there with Whitey and Kathleen.

Her inner beauty shines through and her personality makes everybody feel like they are the most important person in the world. She also knows how to run a business and works her shirt-tail off, seven days a week. My concern for her is that she doesn't have time to play. She only has time to run her business and care for her family. But she is very good at both, and I think the world of her for that.

Renee Kerstetter, who is now married, and a very pretty salesperson, works for the McClanahan Corporation of Pennsylvania. She is a very bright Penn State graduate who has worked her way into this tough business of selling to farm customers. Her commitment to selling to her customers is the theme of her whole being. She and I have sat and talked for hours, and she extracted all the business and selling experiences I have had so she can grow and service her potential customers with professional care.

Her family – mother, father, and sisters – reflect the same qualities every person should enjoy. Now married and expecting her first child, Renee has not missed one beat in her quest for the first prize of selling, and that is acquiring a happy customer. That's the goal of every successful salesperson. If I ever needed another salesperson, Renee would be my choice, as she really has her act together; and she is my friend.

Larry Richers of Professional Dairy Services is a gentleman who everyone in business would be proud to know. He is a professional in every respect and a friend upon whom I can rely. Whenever we are promoting a project, he and I have joined together to sponsor many different events, knowing good and well that we complement one another and have mutual respect for each other. If you want someone who has an outstanding set of business skills and perseverance, it would be Larry. He does his homework and earns his way in this path we call our business life. We spend a lot of time bouncing ideas off of each other to help set in our minds the direction we need to travel.

You know, there are so many people who have impacted my life. It is really difficult to remember all of the names. The blessing of all of the friend, customers, and business acquaintances is a big challenge!

Chapter Thirteen
A Survivor

Every two years, pilots are required to get a flight physical. It was the summer of two thousand and four when I passed the physical. But during the exam, the doctor, who is certified to do pilot physicals, mentioned that he wanted me to schedule an appointment with an urologist, to be on the safe side. It appears that while doing the exam, he noticed that my prostate was enlarged. So, I made an appointment to see Dr. James Iwakiri, a local urologist, a week later.

It was August two thousand and four, my cell phone rang, and it was Dr. Irwikiri calling. He said, "Phil, your PSA is 17, and it should be no higher than 4. I want you in my office tomorrow for a biopsy of your prostrate. The procedure consists of entering your rectum with a device that snips some tissue from your prostrate. It will be used for further study." It was a very painful procedure that had to be done. Twelve biopsies later, they were finished. Now I know what a real pain in the ass feels like.

My cell phone rang. Again it was Dr. Irwakiri. He said he needed to see me and my daughters in his office as soon as possible.

A few days later, as we sat in his office, he told us that I had late stage cancer. I became numb. I'm not sure that I heard all of the options, but he explained that I had better get my things in order, as my chances of recovery were less than fifty percent. It was hard for this to stick in my very confused brain. Surgery was very risky, but in my case, it was the only option. It was scheduled that week.

After surgery, I was in unbearable pain. I don't remember much of the next two weeks except for the incredible pain, and I felt very sick. I thought the chemo treatments were really more than I could handle; however, they were necessary.

During the ensuing six months, I lost ninety two pounds. I couldn't eat or drink. The doctor had surgically removed my prostrate and all the surrounding lymph nodes. After three months, my PSA had gone down to zero. It was a very good sign. However, he chose to continue chemo for the next three years, at three-month intervals. Of course, each time I received chemo, my PSA was checked. It remained at zero. My final chemo treatment was in August of two thousand and seven. I continue to have a checkup every four months so as to make sure I don't have some reoccurrence. Dr Irwakiri will declare me cancer-free after seven years.

It was the first week of January two thousand and six, on a Saturday night. I was watching the news and got this urge to urinate, but I couldn't. After about a half hour of trying over and over again, I finally called the doctor at the clinic. He told me to get to Sacred Heart Hospital as soon as possible. I remember it being very foggy out as I drove myself to the emergency room. When I finally arrived at the emergency room, the doctor was there to meet me. He inserted a tube through my stomach into the bladder to relieve the pressure. Then he placed a catheter through this opening and sent me home. I need surgery again to open my urinary canal. The procedure was done a week or so later. From then on, my life seemed to be normal, whatever normal means.

During my recovery from prostrate cancer, another medical emergency occurred. I was working at the Farm Progress Days in July of two thousand and six. It was the one near Sheboygan Falls, Wisconsin. One night, as I lay in bed, I couldn't get my breath. That had happened about three or four times before. I realized something was wrong. So I got up and got dressed. I went out to my car, punched in the nearest hospital on the GPS (Global Positioning System) and off I went to the emergency room. All night long, the staff ran a number of tests on me, concluding that I was suffering from congestive heart failure. For the next two days I worked the farm show. I felt just fine, except for being a little tired.

Once at home, my daughter, Suzanne, a nurse in the cardiac unit at Marshfield, suggested I visit with a cardiologist at the Marshfield Clinic. She lined up a visit with a doctor friend of hers, Dr. Rezkalla, and told me that he was the best there was. I remember him saying to me, "Phil, let's not guess what is wrong." So I was sent to the Cath Lab for a heart catheterization.

When I returned to my hospital room, there stood both my daughters, Catherine and Suzanne, crying like crazy. Suzanne said, "Dad, you have to have heart bypass surgery. You can't live without it."

So once again, Suzanne talked to her friend, Dr. Hope Mackey, one of the best heart surgeons. The night before surgery, Father Keith Apfelbeck gave me my last rites again. They performed the bypass surgery on July twenty fifth. Two thousand and six. I don't remember much about it, but was later told that I was not the best patient. I remember overhearing in the critical care unit that all my family members stood vigil throughout the many hours.

After the surgery, I complained a lot and was generally difficult to get along with. Yes, I was a real pain in the butt. The good news was that I got to meet many of the people my daughter, Suzanne, works with and, of course, many of my other daughter, Catherine's, friends.

The following Saturday, five days after the surgery, I was discharged from the hospital. Suzanne took me to my home and stayed with me for the first week. Catherine cared for me the following week, and over the course of the following weeks, many other family and friends took excellent care of me and helped in so many ways.

My brother-in-law, Brian, took me to physical therapy. And my good friend, Rich Boie, helped with caretaking chores around the house and made sure I had what I needed. Except for walking the stairs, I didn't follow many of the suggestions, especially the special diet the girls had set up for me.

My recovery was punctuated by a number of setbacks and was painfully slow. I was in excruciating pain. One day as I was walking up the steps at church, I had this pain in my chest. It turned out that my lungs were filling with fluid, and so I had to have a couple of lung infusions. I was not able to drive, so I relied on neighbors and friends to take me to get groceries, and go to doctor's visits and church. I wasn't to drive for a month, but on the thirty first day of my recovery, I got into the car and drove.

I remember asking why this was happening to me. Was I aging and not accepting it? Was this normal? I did give up a few times. I didn't participate in life, didn't turn on the television, answer the phone or think about tomorrow. I even gave up on the idea of ever flying again. But that all changed when I walked to the edge of the runway. I said to myself, "Phil, you can beat this."

I remember Dr. Mackey said that she performs two of these bypass surgeries each day, four days a week. She does eight surgeries per week, and there are five surgeons on staff at this hospital alone. That is forty surgeries per week. I remember her saying to me that sooner or later, if people live long enough, everyone will have bypass surgery. A friend of mine, Jerry Rademaker, was at the hospital at the same time having the very same surgery. And within four months time, I knew four of my family and friends who had the surgery as well.

In mid-January, two thousand and eight, I started to get cloudy vision in my right eye, and by early February, I was totally blind in that eye. I worked the Tulare, California Farm Show in early February, and then on February eighteenth, I had eye surgery at the Marshfield Hospital to correct my loss of vision. The surgery took about four to four and a half hours and consisted of removing bone matter around my eye socket to give room for the muscles to expand and relieve the pressure on my optic nerve. Dr. Cancel and Dr. Boyle operated together, and after a night's stay in the hospital, I was able to see again. My eyesight has improved since the surgery, but it was not without some concerns because of another incident.

It was Easter, Saturday night, March twenty second two thousand and eight, I had gone to my in-laws, Joyce and Vern Whirry, in Eau Claire, Wisconsin. I had taken with me Janet and Brian Soli, Joan's other sister and her husband who live in Stanley. Wisconsin, not far from me. We met my daughter, Suzanne, and her children for an Easter meal. After supper, my grandson, Neil and I went to do some shopping for something that I needed. When we returned, it was pretty late. So, around eight o'clock that evening, Janet, Brian, and I left for home.

I was driving east on Highway twenty nine, with the cruise control on and I must have hit some black ice. It propelled our vehicle into the median where there was a crossover. The vehicle rolled about five times forward. I was pinned in the vehicle for almost thirty or forty minutes, which gave me some time to reflect on my life and what had just happened.

I thought about how fortunate I was to still be living. My injuries were cuts and bruises and a severed artery in my head. I was taken to the emergency room along with my in-laws, Brian and Janet. A great deal of the night was spent getting my head fixed up with thirty-three staples. But as life would have it, even tragic incidents have their lighter moments. When they were cutting off my blood-soaked clothing, one of the nurses in the emergency room said, "Hey Phil, you have a Kentucky roadmap stuck to your butt."

When she told me that, it struck my funny bone and I said, "Well, welcome to Kentucky."

The rest of the night was spent patching me up, and after tests and x-rays, I was discharged in the care of my daughter, Suzanne. Being at home for a couple of days and licking my wounds, trying to regain my strength, I thought of an idea. I thought of having a gathering of friends and family. I decided to call it the Five-B Party, which stands for Beer, Brandy, Brats, Buns, and Beans. I sent out emails, flyers, and called people. Sure enough, the following Saturday, a week after the accident, we had one big party at the "The Salty Dog." There was a polka band and lots of food and drink.

People came from all over, and we just had a nice "I survived it" party. It was a lot of fun and it made the tragedy of the car wreck seem to go away. We focused on celebrating life.

Chapter Fourteen
Upon Reflection

This book is really a celebration of life. I don't remember exactly how it came about, but way back when, the grandkids and Joan were filling out one of those family books about events and the like. They said to her, "We know while we've been here what you do and what you are all about and what happened, but we don't know anything about your past. We can't carry on this whole family circle because we don't know what it is." And that's what this book is all about.

When I went skiing alone one time, I had a lot of time on my hands and decided to write this book. Then I stopped and went to Florida for a couple of weeks and worked on it again. The more that I got done, the more things I remembered to write down. Then I felt an obligation to get it done. You don't leave stuff undone; you just do it. And that's what it is all about. I started it; I've got to finish it.

I've found that writing this memoir has been like painting. You start with one wall in here. Then, you look at the other walls and realize that you have to paint the entire place. I could go on and on for years and years and never remember everything.

Last year, I went to "Sun and Fun" with my sister-in-law, Joyce and her husband, Vern. I took them with me to Orlando, Florida. We stayed with my nephew, Mike and his family in St. Cloud, Florida, and we had a ball. Joyce and Vern had never been to Florida, so it was a totally new experience for them. After three days at Lakeland, we drove south to Fort Lauderdale, Florida, where I had rented a couple of condominiums. We had awesome views, fished on the drift boats, and just hung out at the pool and beach.

I would usually make us a big old breakfast for us in my condo. It was so much fun for me to share this with them. To give people something they had never had before and watch them enjoy it is the greatest feeling. These are the kinds of things that keep me going.

But it hasn't been easy to be alone, without Joan. Being alone sucks. It sucks for two reasons;

first, you don't have anyone with whom to share your day-to-day life. The second reason is that events are not fun at all anymore. You get invited to graduation, a wedding, or other events and you go alone; internally you feel everybody is looking at you.

Finding someone to share my life with was the greatest pleasure. Joan was my partner in life, my soul mate. I suppose I could meet someone new to share my life with, but I have only one wife and am happy with that. So the answer is "No." I won't get married again.

I've got some other things going on to keep me busy. Not long ago I had this dream, which I put into action. I plan on selling off some of my property along the grass airstrip. I've done the surveying, and I've decided to sell four or five lots for people to build homes on, with hangers for their small aircraft. It will be a small community of pilots. Each property will have access to the airstrip right outside their hangar. They can fly wherever they wish, and upon return, they will be at home. I have lived my dream at my North Fork Airport for over thirty years. I want to offer that same opportunity to other pilots.

In February of two thousand and seven, I got a little puppy, four weeks old. She is a yellow lab, and I named her Daisy. She has since become a member of my family. She is the one that keeps me company around home. She's grown into an adult now and lives both inside and outside. She has the run of the house; in fact, she sleeps in my bed at night. When I am traveling on trips for more than a day, she stays at home, and I find someone to care for her. She is probably the best cared for dog in North America. She is a friend to everyone and is a joy for me to have around the house.

But life is not just quiet times with Daisy. I refuse to grow up or grow old. My inner being fights it. I don't believe those guys who think there is a time when you have to throw in the towel. I am a senior citizen, but I don't think that way. Most of the things I do are more youthful activities than those of other senior citizens – like going to Oktoberfest with Whitey. When you get Whitey and me together, you are going to laugh your ass off. You won't believe what happened at the bobsled event. I laughed so hard I almost cried.

Oktoberfest in Chippewa Falls is a German music and food event. There are several tents set up for dancing, food, drinking, and other things. I was joined by Whitey, his daughter, and three or four of their girlfriends. They stayed here in "The Love Shack," and then we all headed off to Oktoberfest. I was still nursing a broken ankle that I acquired, complements of my "Harley , but I went. Pretty soon I saw Whitey talking to a group of people, and he was pointing at me. Right after that, a woman comes over and says that she would like to shake my hand.

She says, "Congratulations. I think that is just awesome that you folks stopped here on the way to the training grounds."

I said, "Thank you so much."

And so she walks away and Whitey starts laughing.

I said, "What in the god-damn hell is going on here."

"Oh," he said, "I just told her that this is the woman's Olympic bobsled team and their coach."

I said, "What? You dumb bastard."

Well anyway, pretty soon this guy comes over and says, "Hey, my wife said that you are the coach from the nineteen eighty six bobsled team and you've got your new team here, and you are on your way from Florida to go training in Minnesota."

I go, "Yeah."

"I want to shake your hand. You seem to be regular people and having a lot of fun. Anyway I just want to thank you for stopping at this event," he said. He was one of the officials.

I said, "Jesus Christ, Whitey."

He said, "Well, we gotta have some fun."

And all of the girls joined in on the fun. They had this band playing called "Barefoot Becky". Becky was the lead singer, and she was barefoot. She comes over to us and said, "Welcome to Chippewa Falls. It is great to have you guys here."

And then they got on the loudspeaker and introduced me as the coach and Whitey the manager of the nineteen eighty six, women's Olympic bobsled team. Pretty soon this little old lady comes over to Whitey and says, "Sir, I need to talk with you."

Whitey says," Yes ma'am, what can I do for you?"

"I'm in the upholstery and awning business and things like that and I understand that you guys are the Olympic bobsled team. How many sleds do you have?"

Whitey goes, "Well, we actually have three, two we practice with and one for the competition."

"Well, she says, "I'll tell you what; it would be an honor for me to provide you with bobsled covers at no charge whatsoever."

Whitey responds, "Well, you know ma'am, we get offers like this all of the time, and we'd love to do it. But you know how the Olympic committee is, so strict on their rules and regulations."

He was bullshitting these people something bad. And he continued, "It would be an honor to accept, but we just can't do that. But thank you so kindly for your offer."

And we got more beer coming our way. People were buying us beer all night long. And guys wanted to dance with the girls.

We were riding home and I said to Whitey, "You SOB."

Now it is a running joke because Missy will call up and say, "Hey coach. We got a new brakeman for the bobsled team."

And I say, "Don't be recruiting!"

As I think about all of my friendships, I think that maybe the wonderful people I've mentioned in this book relate to me because of my outgoing personality, not to mention that I'm funnier than hell, especially when I drink a dozen beers, and I can dance like crazy. Maybe they see spending time with me as a release from their own lives. Sometimes people find it hard to believe that I can be non-stressed. What is there to worry about? When the wind is blowing really hard and lightening is cracking everywhere, can you do anything about it? No. There are a lot of things that you can do, but to recognize the things that you can't do anything about is crucial. The only thing you can change is your attitude.

This is a snapshot of my life. It is but a small description of my journey, and it is far from complete in terms of details and events. It is a broad picture of the various stages of the road I've walked. My family, children, and grandchildren, relatives and friends have made my life a charmed life. My daughters are a huge part of my life, both of them, Catherine and Suzanne, and I am so proud of them. It is hard to imagine that I deserve it all.

It is my dream that all people enjoy a marriage that lasts forever, family and friends who support and love them, and great health. These are the things I believe make for a fulfilling life.

To those who have been a part of my life, I say, "I love you" and "Thank You." For without people, all the material things have no meaning. The experiences that are tied to friends and family are the things that are most important in life. Need I say more?

No.

Life is not about waiting for the storm's to pass, it's about learning how to dance in the rain.

The journey continues.